Warrior • 55

Imperial Japanese Naval Aviator 1937–45

Osamu Tagaya • Illustrated by John White

A CIP catalogue record for this book is available from the British Library

ISBN 1 84176 385 3

Editor: Tom Lowres
Design: Ken Vail Graphic Design, Cambridge, UK
Index by Alan Rutter
Originated by The Electronic Page Company, Cwmbran, UK
Printed in China through World Print Ltd.

03 04 05 06 07 10 9 8 7 6 5 4 3 2 1

For a catalogue of all books published by Osprey Military and Aviation please contact:

Osprey Direct UK, P.O. Box 140, Wellingborough, Northants, NN8 2FA, UK
E-mail: info@ospreydirect.co.uk

Osprey Direct USA, c/o MBI Publishing, P.O. Box 1, 729 Prospect Ave, Osceola, WI 54020, USA
E-mail: info@ospreydirectusa.com

www.ospreypublishing.com

Artist's note

Readers may care to note that the original paintings from which the color plates in this book were prepared are available for private sale. All reproduction copyright whatsoever is retained by the Publishers. All enquiries should be addressed to:

John White,
5107-C Monroe Road,
Charlotte,
North Carolina 28205,
704-537-7717,
USA

The Publishers regret that they can enter into no correspondence upon this matter.

Author's acknowledgments

My sincere thanks go to the following individuals for their kind help, advice and support in the preparation of this title: Richard Dunn, Robert C. Mikesh, Gary Nila, Henry Sakaida, Yoshio Tagaya, and Edward M. Young. My heartfelt thanks also go to the editorial staff at Osprey Publishing for their unlimited patience during the long preparation of this book.

Editor's note

All photographs are from the author's collection unless otherwise stated.
All references to education levels in the text refer to the prewar and wartime system unless specifically noted otherwise.

CONTENTS

IMPERIAL JAPANESE NAVAL AVIATOR 1937–45

HISTORY

In the beginning, pilot training in the Imperial Japanese Navy (IJN) was open only to commissioned officers. As a new and largely unproven field, however, aviation provided little opportunity for career advancement to graduates of the naval academy. With the realization that other sources of recruitment would be needed to expand the ranks of naval aviation quickly, pilot training was made available to non-commissioned officers on a trial basis for the first time in March 1914. With the success of this program, recruitment of aviators from the navy's non-commissioned and enlisted ranks was permanently established in May 1920. Within a few years the number of non-commissioned officers and enlisted airmen came to outnumber commissioned officer pilots significantly. Ultimately, unlike the air forces of the West, in which the number of commissioned officer pilots remained predominant, the Japanese air forces, and that of the IJN in particular, came to rely primarily on non-commissioned and enlisted ranks to fill the sky. Typically only a handful of commissioned officers would be assigned to active flight duty in any unit, normally leading formations down to *chutai* (nine planes) and sometimes *shotai* (three planes) size. All remaining positions were usually held by warrant officers, petty officers and enlisted airmen. As attrition took its toll in China and the Pacific, and as the expansion of training programs proved far too slow, non-commissioned ranks, by necessity, came to assume ever higher levels of tactical command, routinely leading formations of *chutai* size and sometimes larger by the mid-war years. In the Imperial Japanese Navy it was the non-commissioned ranks that produced the largest number of fighter aces and those with the highest scores. It was they who flew the most number of bombing missions. It was they who did most of the flying, the fighting, and the dying.

While the substance of commissioned officer pilot training differed little from that of other ranks, the privileges and responsibilities of commissioned status clearly set those men apart in a service imbued with elitist attitudes. This book endeavors to describe the experiences of a

Three trainee pilots in full flight gear watch intently through binoculars as one of their colleagues takes a turn in the air.

Pilot briefing before the mission. The men synchronize their watches on a signal from the mission leader. Both pre-mission and post-mission briefings typically took place outdoors in the IJN Air Service throughout the China War and Pacific War. This photograph, taken during the early stages of the China War, shows the pilots wearing early-style flight goggles with flat lenses and straight upper rims.

typical IJN airman and will therefore concentrate on the non-commissioned and enlisted ranks to the exclusion of their more privileged commissioned superiors.

In June 1930 the non-commissioned and enlisted pilots' program, previously known by the cumbersome name of *Hiko Jutsu Renshu Sei* (Flying Technique Trainee Program), was formally renamed. Products of this program were thereafter known as *Soh-ju Renshu Sei* (Pilot Trainee) or *Sohren* for short. Shortly before this, in 1928, a new avenue of non-commissioned pilot recruitment had been opened that drew directly from the civilian population. This was the *Hiko Yoka Renshu Sei* (Flight Reserve Trainee Program) or *Yokaren* (the prefix *Hiko* was added in 1936), and the first class under this program began their training in June 1930.

Throughout the 1930s the *Sohren* and *Yokaren* were the two main gateways of enlisted airmen recruitment in the IJN. The *Sohren* program was open, through competitive written examination, to any non-commissioned officer or enlisted seaman already in the navy's ranks. The *Yokaren*, however, drew directly from civilian boys aged 15 to 17 who had completed higher primary school, or the equivalent of second-year middle school, under the prewar education system. It also required a competitive entrance examination. Successful candidates were placed in

Yokaren cadets undergoing semaphore training. The Flight Reserve Trainee Program emphasized all aspects of navy life before proceeding to flight instruction. (via Edward M. Young)

a training program originally lasting three years (shortened to two and a half years following the outbreak of the China War and eventually to under two years following the start of the Pacific War) which concentrated on basic education and training in the ways of the navy. The *Sohren* program, on the other hand, moved quickly on to actual flight training and lasted approximately a year in total as the men under this program had already received basic training in other branches of the navy before becoming pilot trainees.

Up to the end of World War II the Japanese education system was modelled on the German *gymnasium* system and consisted of the following levels: primary school: six years (students who did not go on to middle school could elect, instead, to attend higher primary school, which required two years beyond the six years of primary school); middle school: five years; high school: three years; university: three years.

Following the end of the World War II, the Japanese education system was thoroughly reorganized and remodeled on the American system as follows: primary school: six years; middle school: three years; high school: three years; university: four years (i.e. undergraduate college. Education beyond this level involved graduate-level university degrees.)

As the demand for pilots grew during the course of the decade, new avenues of recruitment were established. An effort to create a pool of reserve officer pilots with university education began in November 1934 with the *Koku Yobi Gakusei* (Air Reserve Student) Program, which drew young men who had graduated from universities and professional schools (under age 26 in the case of universities; under 24 in the case of professional schools). The program was limited initially to members of the navy-sponsored marine division of the Nippon Student Aviation League, a sports flying association with chapters in graduate-level schools throughout the country. Resistance by the naval academy elite to opening the floodgate of commissions to reservists ensured that the program remained very restricted in the years before the outbreak of the Pacific War. The first class admitted only five students, Class No. 8 of April 1941 counted only 43 in its ranks, and Class No. 11 of September 1942 still only had 85. It was not until 1943 that the program was greatly expanded and new programs instituted to cover students attending high school (roughly equivalent to undergraduate college in the postwar education system). This was in sharp contrast to the United States, which by 1940 had established a major program to train men of college age as aviators, thus creating an army of citizen soldier pilots who brought ultimate victory in the air to their nation during World War II.

Despite the narrow-minded views of traditionalists in the IJN, there was no denying the urgency of expanding pilot training as the world drifted towards war in the latter half of the 1930s. May 1937 saw the establishment of a new program drawing on civilian men between the ages of 16 and 19 who had completed three and a half years of their middle school education (equivalent to the middle of first-year high school in the American-based postwar education system.) The first class of this program reported for duty in September 1937, shortly after the outbreak of the undeclared war with China. These men were designated

The cadets listen intently to a classroom lecture. Note the small oval name tags on their work uniforms. (via Edward M. Young)

Ko-shu Hiko Yoka Renshu Sei (A-class Flight Reserve Trainee) and they came to constitute by far the largest category of air cadets. Simultaneously the original *Yokaren* were redesignated *Otsu-shu Hiko Yoka Renshu Sei* (B-class Flight Reserve Trainee). In October 1940 the old *Sohren* system, which drew directly from men already in the navy, was phased out and replaced by *Hei-shu Hiko Yoka Renshu Sei* (C-class Flight Reserve Trainee).

Reflecting the higher level of education with which they entered the navy, *Ko Yokaren* spent only a year and a half (later shortened to a year or less in the latter half of the Pacific War) in basic education and training before moving on to flight training. *Hei Yokaren,* already products of naval training in other branches of the navy, required only a couple of months of basic education before progressing to flight training.

Flight training itself was now standardized for all three classes of *Yokaren* and was known as the *Hiko Renshu Sei* (Flight Trainee) or *Hiren* program. In contrast, flight trainees who were graduates of the naval academy were known as *Hiko Gakusei* (Flight Student).

Sohren training was based at Kasumigaura *Kokutai* near Japan's second largest lake of the same name northeast of Tokyo in Ibaraki Prefecture. The program was later expanded to other bases including Tsukuba *Kokutai* in 1938 and Yatabe *Kokutai* in 1939.

Yokaren were originally based at Yokosuka, but with this oldest of IJN air bases becoming increasingly crowded, they moved to new facilities on the shores of Lake Kasumigaura, just north of the old Kasumigaura air base in March 1939, becoming known as the *Yokaren* Division of Kasumigaura *Kokutai.* When the *Hei Yokaren,* heirs to the old *Sohren* program, started in October 1940, they also moved here from the old Kasumigaura. Then, with the completion of headquarters facilities on the shores of the lake, the *Yokaren* Division became an independent *kokutai* in its own right in November 1940 and was designated Tsuchiura *Kokutai*, taking its name from the nearest large town just north of the old Kasumigaura *Ku*.

The ranks of the *Yokaren* grew steadily during 1941 and 1942, but only two *kokutai* were added to the program in these years: Iwakuni *Kokutai*, first activated in December 1939, which added *Yokaren* training to its mission from November 1941 (later phased out in October 1943); and Mie *Kokutai* which was formed as a *Yokaren* unit from the start in August 1942. It was not until 1943 that the program saw major growth as selection standards were reduced. In 1944 educational requirements for entry were lowered. By the end of the Pacific War some 20 *kokutai* were focused on churning out *Yokaren* by the thousand. But these men were a far cry from the small group of highly skilled airmen that the system had produced in the prewar years.

In the spring of 1943 the *Hei Yokaren* Program was phased out and replaced by the *Toku* (Special) *Otsu Yokaren* Program, which began in April of that year. This was an accelerated five- to seven-month course for men drawn from the more mature ranks of *Otsu Yokaren*. But this program, in turn, was closed following the start of the last class in October 1944. In the previous month *Yokaren* started to be diverted to mission roles other than aircrew, as fuel and aircraft shortages began to have an impact. These "wingless" *Yokaren* typically became aircraft mechanics or communications troops. September 1944 had also seen the first *Yokaren* graduates destined directly for suicide sorties. The present work is not intended to cover the *kamikaze* experience, but such was the tragic fate of many young IJN airmen in the closing months of the war.

On 1 March 1945 all flight training was officially halted. All available aviation fuel had to be used for combat or held in reserve for use against the expected invasion of the Home Islands. All aircraft were now on combat status. When the suicide units ran out of first-line aircraft, they went out in trainers. When there were no more trainers, the hapless *Yokaren* prepared to sacrifice themselves in any way they could: in *Kaiten* human torpedoes, *Shinyo* suicide motor boats and in *Koryu* midget submarines. During the 1937–45 war, some 18,900

Telegraph training. (via Edward M. Young)

Yokaren of all classes were killed in action out of 241,463 entering trainees. (This figure does not include the old *Sohren* program prior to its incorporation into the *Hei*-Class *Yokaren*, or any of the commissioned officer programs.)

In retrospect the IJN maintained a rigorously exclusive policy in its aviator programs for far too long. The *Otsu Yokaren* admitted little more than 200 men annually up until 1938, and class size did not exceed 1,000 until May 1941. *Otsu Yokaren* Class No. 19 of December 1942 still had only 1,500 recruits. The figure then suddenly jumped to 2,951 in the following Class No. 20 of May 1943. Among the *Ko Yokaren*, by far the largest of the *Yokaren* programs, annual class sizes remained in the 250–260 range for most of the China War period. Numbers did not exceed 1,000 until Class No. 10 of April 1942. A year later Class No. 12 counted 3,215, divided into three groups. The figure then exploded to almost 28,000 in Class No. 13, divided into two groups of October and December 1943.

The transition in the IJN from a system geared to producing a highly select group of airmen to a mass recruitment system not only came too late, but also came too abruptly. The Imperial Navy's cadre of pre-Pacific War veterans that had attacked Pearl Harbor and conquered Southeast Asia with such stunning speed and awesome displays of aerial skill was, for all its prowess, a fragile force lacking in depth. Attrition thinned its ranks in the great carrier battles of 1942 and in the grinding combat over Guadalcanal in the latter half of that year. The numbers of pre-Pacific War veterans grew fewer still during the attrition battles fought over the Solomon Islands and New Guinea during 1943, and their replacements arrived in front-line units with increasingly less experience and skill. Then in the great showdown with the US Pacific Fleet in the Philippine Sea in June 1944 the products of the greatly expanded wartime training programs were shown to be woefully inferior to their American counterparts. Committed to battle before their training was complete even by the diluted Japanese standards then prevailing, and confronted by an enemy armed with superior fighters manned by more experienced pilots, and warships with formidable anti-aircraft defences and effective radar, the once proud airmen of the IJN were shot down in droves with little to show for their sacrifice. Thereafter, descent into desperation led ultimately to the suicide sorties of the Special Attack Corps.

Given Japan's fundamental folly in initiating a war with an enemy ten times its size both in manpower and industrial might, the final outcome of the Pacific War would probably have been the same regardless of Japanese efforts. Nonetheless, had a larger reserve of adequately trained airmen been established earlier, the collapse in the effectiveness of Japan's aerial efforts might not have been so sudden or dramatic. But even in the midst of defeat, in the final months of the Pacific War, the few surviving veterans could still dazzle friend and foe alike with their aerial skills as they fought their lonely battles against a swarm of enemies. Theirs was the true legacy of the Imperial Japanese Naval airman; a member of a small, elite band of brethren, trained to perfection and seasoned in combat, who, for a brief moment in history, ruled the skies over Asia and the Pacific as the most formidable naval aviators in the world.

CHRONOLOGY

June 1 1930	Flying Technique Trainee Program redesignated Pilot Trainee Program (*Sohren*) First class under new *Yokaren* Program begins
July 7 1937	Marco Polo Bridge incident leads to general undeclared war with China
September 1 1937	First class of new A-class *Yokaren* (*Ko Yokaren*) Program begins Original *Yokaren* redesignated B-class Yokaren (*Otsu Yokaren*)
March 1 1939	Yokaren Program transferred from Yokosuka Kokutai to Kasumigaura *Kokutai Yokaren* Division
October 1 1940	First class of C-class Yokaren (*Hei Yokaren*) begins, and replaces old *Sohren* Program
November 15 1940	Kasumigaura *Kokutai Yokaren* Division becomes independent as Tsuchiura *Kokutai*
December 7 (8) 1941	Attack on Pearl Harbor. Pacific War begins
June 4–7 1942	Battle of Midway
August 7 1942	Guadalcanal campaign begins
February 1–7 1943	Japanese withdraw from Guadalcanal
April 1 1943	First class of Special B-class *Yokaren* (*Toku Otsu Yokaren*) Program begins
June 19–20 1944	Battle of the Philippine Sea
October 25 1944	First successful sortie of Kamikaze Special Attack Corps
March 1 1945	Flight training in IJN terminated
April 1 1945	Battle for Okinawa begins
August 6 & 9 1945	Atomic bombs fall on Hiroshima and Nagasaki
August 15 1945	Japan surrenders

RECRUITMENT AND TRAINING

The following description of trainee life relates to the original *Yokaren* program in the prewar years which became *Otsu Yokaren* following the institution of the *Ko Yokaren* program in 1937. The experience was typical of all who went through any of the *Yokaren* programs. The *Ko* and *Hei Yokaren* simply endured it for shorter periods. It should be noted that the entire recruitment and training process as described here was speeded up following the start of the China War in 1937 and more so following the start of the Pacific War at the end of 1941.

Hiren **trainees prepare to go up in Type 3 Primary Trainers. Although originally powered by a 130hp Mitsubishi Mongoose radial as the K2Y1, the major production version, as shown here, was the K2Y2, powered by a 160hp Hitachi Kamikaze.**

Following primary training, the pilot trainees graduated onto the Type 93 Intermediate Trainer. The undercarriage version was given the short-code designation K5Y1. Trainers in the IJN came to be known affectionately as *akatombo* (*"red dragonfly"*), a reference to the overall orange-yellow finish they came to sport from 1939 onwards.

A variety of factors motivated teenage boys to enlist in the air service of the Imperial Japanese Navy, but by far the greatest for many was their love of aeroplanes. Growing up in the golden age of aviation between the two world wars, many were imbued with the glamor of man's conquest of the air and the mystique of flight. But during the 1930s aviation and submarines were considered hazardous duty in the IJN and written parental permission was needed before applying to these branches of the service. This was often given with great reluctance by parents concerned for the safety of their sons, acquiescence coming only after loud and persistent efforts by the eager young lads. Sometimes permission was not forthcoming at all. In their determination to become naval airmen, it was not unheard of for some boys to forge their parents' seal on the application documents.

Having overcome this first hurdle, the young aspiring naval airman faced a highly competitive written examination held once a year in the prewar years (twice or more from 1938 onwards) in centers all across the country. With barely 200 individuals or fewer accepted out of more than 20,000 applicants each year during most of the prewar years, the odds against induction were often more than 100 to one. Together with applicants for other branches of the navy, our aspiring airman would first take a 15-minute test in mathematics consisting of 50 questions. This was followed by a 20-minute test in reading and writing, also consisting of 50 questions. As the tests were completed the examiners would call out a list of names. Our aspiring airman would be disheartened when his name was not called, only to be relieved shortly after by the discovery that it was those whose names had been called who had failed to make the grade. Those aiming for other branches of the navy required lower scores, but aspirants for the air service needed an average score of 85 percent.

Next came a thorough physical examination, which included measurements of height, weight, chest size, eyesight, hearing, reflexes, lung capacity, muscular strength and blood pressure. Here again a large number of boys were dismissed. Successful passage of the physical examination was followed by a 40-minute aptitude test and an oral examination before the head examiner. With that the first round of examinations was over, and final results were posted about two months later. This was followed by instructions to report for a second round of examinations that would last three to five days. This took place at a major *kokutai* in each naval district. For the *Yokaren* in prewar years the place of examination was Yokosuka *Kokutai*, later moved to Tsuchiura. This second round concentrated on a more detailed physical examination and more probing aptitude tests, both written and physical. With successful passage of the second round came formal induction into the navy *Yokaren* program and the exchange of civilian clothing for the traditional blue and white sailor uniform of the Imperial Navy with the rank of Airman 4th Class. (See the table below for an explanation of non-commissioned rank nomenclature in the IJN air service.)

May 1 1929–May 31 1941

Rank/class	Full rank in Japanese	English translation & abbreviation
WO	*Koku Hei Socho*	Air Chief Petty Officer (ACPO)
NCO	*Itto Koku Heiso*	Air Petty Officer 1st Class (APO 1/C)
	Nito Koku Heiso	Air Petty Officer 2nd Class (APO 2/C)
	Santo Koku Heiso	Air Petty Officer 3rd Class (APO 3/C)
Enlisted	*Itto Kokuhei*	Airman 1st Class (A 1/C)
	Nito Kokuhei	Airman 2nd Class (A 2/C)
	Santo Kokuhei	Airman 3rd Class (A 3/C)
	Yonto Kokuhei	Airman 4th Class (A 4/C)

June 1 1941–October 31 1942

Koku (Air) designation replaced by *Hiko* (Flight). All else remained as before

Rank/class	Full rank in Japanese	English translation & abbreviation
WO	*Hiko Hei Socho*	Flight Chief Petty Officer (FCPO)
NCO	*Itto Hiko Heiso*	Flight Petty Officer 1st Class (FPO 1/C)
	Nito Hiko Heiso	Flight Petty Officer 2nd Class (FPO 2/C)
	Santo Hiko Heiso	Flight Petty Officer 3rd Class (FPO 3/C)
Enlisted	*Itto Hikohei*	Flyer 1st Class (F 1/C)
	Nito Hikohei	Flyer 2nd Class (F 2/C)
	Santo Hikohei	Flyer 3rd Class (F 3/C)
	Yonto Hikohei	Flyer 4th Class (F 4/C)

November 1 1942–end of war

The system changed to bring it into line with army nomenclature. The term "Flight Petty Officer 1st Class" was replaced by "Superior Flight Petty Officer" and other NCO ranks were renumbered accordingly, thus eliminating FPO 3/C rank. The terms "Flyer 1st Class" and "Flyer 2nd Class" were replaced by "Chief Flyer" and "Superior Flyer" respectively and other enlisted ranks renumbered accordingly, thus eliminating F 3/C and F 4/C ranks

Rank/class	Full rank in Japanese	English translation & abbreviation
WO	*Hiko Hei Socho*	Flight Chief Petty Officer (FCPO)
NCO	*Joto Hiko Heiso*	Superior Flight Petty Officer (SFPO)
	Itto Hiko Heiso	Flight Petty Officer 1st Class (FPO 1/C)
	Nito Hiko Heiso	Flight Petty Officer 2nd Class (FPO 2/C)
Enlisted	*Hiko Heicho*	Chief Flyer (CF)
	Joto Hikohei	Superior Flyer (SF)
	Itto Hikohei	Flyer 1st Class (F 1/C)
	Nito Hikohei	Flyer 2nd Class (F 2/C)

During the period covered in this book, the rank system for non-commissioned IJN airmen was changed on three separate occasions. This has often been the source of some confusion for followers of the subject. It is hoped that the tables on p.12 will provide clarification.

The main event of the first day for the new recruits was the induction ceremony, an address by the base commander who peered down at them from the drill platform as they stood to attention on the parade ground. The day following induction saw the start of a new life for these 15- to 17-year-old boys. Any glamorous notions they held of soon becoming airmen were quickly dispelled by a routine of strict regimentation and often brutal discipline. The next three years would be filled more with instruction in basic subjects and exposure to other branches of the navy than to the complexities of aeronautics. The *Yokaren* curriculum was designed to raise the educational level of the recruits to that of a middle-school graduate (equivalent to completion of the second-year of American high school under the postwar system), give them basic training and broad exposure to life in naval service, and to instil in them an aggressive fighting spirit as professional warriors of the Imperial Navy. (Note: In the case of *Ko Yokaren* who had already finished first semester, fourth year of their middle school education at the time of their entry into the navy, the one-and-a-half-year program which they went through also brought their level of education up to the middle-school graduate level.) The first two months of the program (three months following the start of the China War) concentrated exclusively on military drill and ground combat training, aimed at whipping these "soft" civilian boys into shape and giving them at least the outward semblance of Imperial Navy bearing. Corporal punishment was a fact of life in the imperial armed forces, and the naval air service was no exception. Any infraction of the rules, no matter how slight, or any perceived lack of proper "spirit" brought swift retribution from instructors and upper classmen alike. Beatings on the buttocks with baseball bats and fist punches to the face became all too familiar for the new recruits. Following this brutal initiation, the recruits settled into their regular course routine.

Reveille was at 0600 hrs (0500 hrs in summer). Jumping out of their hammocks the recruits had to roll them up tightly, exactly in the prescribed manner, secure them in their individual

A close-up of the instructor giving his last-minute instructions to the trainee through the voice tube.

The trainee listens carefully. Note the listening tube attached to his flight helmet. Both instructor and trainee wear the new "cat's eye" flight goggles with large curved lenses, standard in the IJN for much of the 1937–45 period.

The trainee, now ready to solo, receives last-minute instructions before taking off on his own.

25x30x100cm canvas bags and stow them in netting. In prewar years this was followed by a quick dunk in cold water, even in winter. The recruits then had to rush out to the parade ground and be lined up by 0610 hrs, ready to begin morning callisthenics five minutes later at 0615 hrs, having first faced in the direction of the Imperial Palace and recited the oath of loyalty that Emperor Meiji had given them. Readiness to begin any activity five minutes before the prescribed time was standard procedure in the Imperial Navy. Also, with the exception of marching in unison as a group, life for the young recruits was always on the double. Any recruit caught walking would be sure to receive a quick beating in the interest of "building his character". Morning exercise was followed by a wash and breakfast. After breakfast, which usually consisted of rice mixed with barley, *miso* soup and pickled vegetables, the *Yokaren* would enter their classrooms and spend 45 minutes in self study. Then back they would go to the parade ground and be lined up by 0800 hrs sharp, ready to march back into their respective classrooms by section to start classes at 0815 hrs. Four hours of morning instruction would follow: four classes of 55 minutes each with a five-minute break in between. These five-minute breaks were anything but restful as they often entailed a mad rush for the "head" by hordes of recruits, recalled many a *Yokaren* trainee. With the end of morning classes at 1215 hrs the recruits would return to their barracks for lunch.

At lunch, each section or *han* (consisting of between 12 and 18 men, depending on the total size of the class) would send two or three of their number on mess duty for that particular week to receive their section's food container from the kitchen and distribute the contents to the men in their section. The meal, usually consisting of fish or meat and always accompanied by barley rice and some pickled vegetables, was eaten with members of each section sitting in two rows facing each other on benches across a wooden table about 5m long by 1m wide. One recruit remembers:

> The meal would begin on command from the section leader sitting at one end of the table. Once again it was a rush. Ever conscious of our schedule, we would often wolf down our food, almost swallowing it whole rather than chewing it properly.

Afternoon classes began at 1315 hrs. As in the morning the recruits lined up on the parade ground and marched into class. Three hours of classes would follow, each of similar duration to those of the morning. The last period in the afternoon was normally devoted to physical activity. Saturday afternoons especially were given over to such pursuits as team sports, martial arts and ground combat exercises. Martial arts included *judo* and *kendo.* Sports included boat races and rugby, reflecting the British influence on Japanese naval traditions.

The most precious part of the day for the *Yokaren* followed afternoon classes and supper when they were given one and a half hours of free time. For these growing teenage boys the normal food portions at the three regular daily meals was often not enough. Rushing to the PX for a bowl of *udon* noodles or *shiruko* sweet bean broth with dumplings was a favorite pastime during the free period. But part of this time had also to be reserved for mundane personal chores such as bathing and laundry.

From 1900 hrs to 2145 hrs came the evening study period. The recruits would go back to their classroom to review the day's lessons, do their homework and prepare for the next day. Silence was strictly enforced. One and a half hours into this study session came a 15-minute break in which the students would go out onto the parade ground and practice giving commands at the top of their voices. This would shake off any accumulated drowsiness, and back they would go to their classroom for the remaining hour of study. From there it was back to the barracks to set up their hammocks and be in bed by 2200 hrs (2100 hrs in summer) before evening inspection came around.

The *Yokaren* curriculum covered 30 subjects in all, including algebra, geometry, physics, chemistry, history, geography, literature and composition, Chinese classics, and English. Military subjects included martial arts, ground-combat training, gunnery, communications and aeronautics. There was a slightly higher concentration of aviation-related courses in the second and third years of the program. Students faced failure unless they maintained a grade above 40 in any one subject and an overall average of over 60 in all subjects. In their determination to maintain the necessary grades, many recruits would slip out of their hammocks after lights out in order to continue their studies under some

ABOVE and TOP Unlike the Type 3 Primary Trainer, the Type 93 Intermediate allowed vigorous aerobatics.

Links trainers were used in the IJN to assess flight aptitude before actual flight training commenced.

dim light bulb, or huddle under the blankets with an electric torch, all against regulations of course.

One unique feature of *Yokaren* organization was that a student's academic standing determined his position within his section. The only exception to this was in physical activity such as sports, in which case one's relative position within the section was determined by one's physical size. In all other activities, whether it was classroom seating, sitting at mess hall or lining up and marching on the parade ground, one could tell immediately where someone stood in academic standing by his relative position in the line-up. This relative position was adjusted each year to reflect changes in standing.

Toward the end of their second year in the *Yokaren* program the trainees finally got their first taste of what they had all been waiting for from the very beginning – a chance actually to go up in an aeroplane. For a one-month period they underwent pilot aptitude tests at the controls of an aircraft in actual flight for the first time. Throughout the 1930s and the start of the Pacific War period this was done on the Type 3 Primary Trainer. This was a two-seat, dual-control biplane design derived from the venerable Avro 504 and, in its initial version, was powered by a 130-horsepower Mitsubishi Mongoose 5 cylinder radial engine (short code designation K2Y1). In pre-China War days these flights were conducted at the Tomobe Detachment of Kasumigaura *Ku*, later to become independent as Tsukuba *Kokutai* in December 1938. In the Type 3 the instructor usually sat in the forward cockpit with the trainee sitting behind. The cadets were tested for hand/eye coordination, smoothness of control, and on how well they could maintain straight and level flight as well as their degree of control in basic turning maneuvers. Among the more adept, a lucky few who went on to master take-offs and landings were actually permitted to solo during this period.

(Following the outbreak of the China War, these aptitude flights were conducted before the end of the second year and for a much

Once pilot trainees had mastered solo flight, the next step was formation work. Here a *shotai* of three Type 93s are seen with Mt Fuji in the background. These aircraft are in overall silver dope with red tails, the standard finish for IJN trainers before the overall orange-yellow finish came into use.

Blind flying training made use of a canvas canopy to shield the trainee as he concentrated on his instruments.

shorter period, the trainees having first been tested on Links trainers. During the latter half of the Pacific War, the aptitude flights were conducted a month and a half after initial entry into the trainee program for *Ko Yokaren* and about three months from the beginning for *Otsu Yokaren*, a graphic illustration of the extent to which the whole process became telescoped under the pressures of war.)

As they began the third and last year of their program, the *Yokaren* could look back with pride on having survived the gruelling regime of the last two years. They were now thoroughly inured to the tough routine and they suffered fewer beatings. Indeed, as senior classmen, they took a hand in disciplining incoming recruits and classmen with lower status.

Based on the results of the flight aptitude tests previously conducted, the class was now divided into those selected to become pilots and those who were to become observers. The curriculum now diverged between the two groups, pilots receiving a greater concentration of courses on engine maintenance, while the observer group devoted more attention to communications.

In peacetime the trainees spent the final months of the *Yokaren* program serving aboard a warship of the fleet. This was cut short by the outbreak of the war in China, but was later revived for a time. After three long years under the full prewar program, the successful senior trainees, having survived a wash-out rate typically averaging over 20 per cent, and now recently promoted to Airman 1st Class, finally marched off to graduation. They did so with the lower classmen lined up in attendance and cheering them on, waving their caps in unison in the traditional farewell of the Imperial Navy.

Intermediate training culminated in mass-formation flight and a final test of all the pilot's skills. Until 1940 the trainees were awarded their "wings" rating patches at this point.

FLIGHT TRAINING

Graduation from the *Yokaren* program was followed immediately by assignment to the *Hiko Renshu Sei* or *Hiren* program for actual flight training. In prewar years this was a seven-month course that covered primary and intermediate levels of flight training. Typically the incoming flight training class was divided upon entry into a seaplane section (floatplanes and flying boats) and a land plane section (aircraft with wheeled undercarriages.) The seaplane section operated off the seaplane ramp by the shores of Lake Kasumigaura. For those destined for land planes, entry into the flight training program meant assignment to the air base. Kasumigaura *Kokutai* was the mecca for pilot training in the IJN for most of its history. It was to the airmen of the Imperial Japanese Navy what Pensacola was to their counterparts in the naval air service of the United States.

Kasumigaura *Kokutai* was a short bus ride from the railway station at Tsuchiura. The approach to the main gate of the air base was lined for about 100m by a beautiful row of cherry trees on both sides of the road. Springtime, when the cherry blossoms were in full bloom, provided a magnificent sight, while the air above reverberated all year round with the sound of training aircraft flying circuits around the field. As the recent *Yokaren* graduates walked this path and through the main gate, they did so in the confident belief that through these portals passed "the best damn naval aviators in the world." Throughout the late 1930s and the early months of the Pacific War, this was no idle boast.

The strict regimentation of the *Yokaren* years now gave way to a little more freedom for the flight trainees. Tobacco and liquor were no longer prohibited, and overnight "shore leave" off base from Saturday afternoon to Sunday night was now allowed. As *Yokaren* they had only been allowed off base on Sundays.

Instruction on the Type 3 Primary Trainer now began in earnest. Three trainees would typically be assigned to one instructor, thus assuring generous individual attention for each trainee. Remarkably this ratio remained unchanged until 1940, but suddenly increased thereafter, doubling to six during 1941 at Kasumigaura, and continued to rise during the Pacific War. Half the day, typically mornings, was reserved for actual flight training, while the other half, usually afternoons, was given over to classroom study for which the land plane and seaplane sections came together. Primary flight training included both the rudiments of flight as well as basic aerobatic maneuvers such as loops, rolls, stalls, and spins. Through it all, Mt Tsukuba, rising to the northwest

Over-water navigation was a vital necessity in the IJN Air Service. Here trainees receive instruction in correcting drift during flight over the sea.

above the Kanto Plain, and Mt Fuji, far to the southwest, provided excellent orientation points for the trainees. Most pilots were allowed to solo after logging about ten hours in the air, a red streamer or triangular flag being attached to the trainer's right wing strut or tail to warn other aircraft while the novice exulted in achieving this major milestone in his career.

After two to three months of primary training the *Hiren* trainees would make a transition to the Type 93 Intermediate Trainer. Powered by a 300hp Hitachi *Amakaze* Model 11, 9-cylinder radial engine, this biplane trainer was the mainstay of IJN flight training from the early years of the China War right through to the end of the Pacific War. With over 5,500 built in several versions (short code designation K5Y1 in its wheeled undercarriage version, K5Y2 in its floatplane version) the Type 93 was a most familiar sight at IJN flight training bases. The Allies in World War II gave it the code name "Willow", but it was known affectionately throughout the Imperial Navy by the unofficial nickname *akatombo* or "red dragonfly", a reference to the overall yellow-orange finish sported by all IJN trainers from 1939 onwards. With twice the power and speed of the Type 3 Primary Trainer, the Type 93 Intermediate could engage in vigorous aerobatics. Also in the Type 93 the trainee sat in the forward cockpit, giving him unfettered forward vision and a much greater sense of being in control.

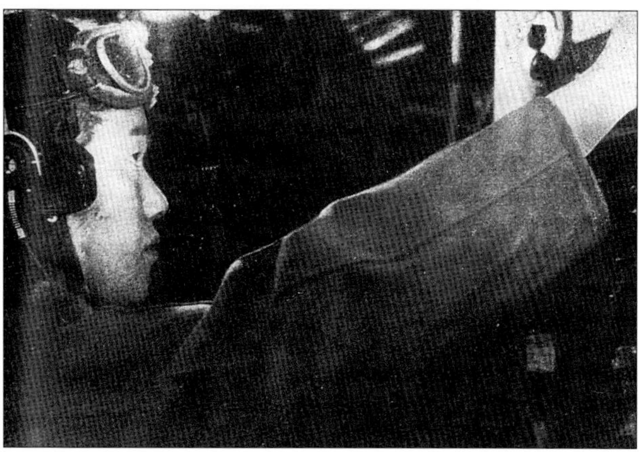

While pilots concentrated on flight skills and engine maintenance, observers concentrated on navigation and communication.

Training now included overland navigation flights away from base, high altitude flights up to 5,000m, formation work and flying on instruments. Toward the end of their intermediate course the trainees were asked on which aircraft type they wished to specialize. As with young pilots throughout the world, the vast majority wanted to be in fighters. They did not always get their wish, of course, but due consideration was given to trainee preference in the assignment of mission roles.

After some five months of intermediate training the *Hiren* program culminated in a final examination in the air which tested all elements of the course including basic flying skills, aerobatics, navigation, and landing in restricted space. The results of this test determined the final grade of the trainees as well as their assignment to a field of specialization.

At this point the flight trainees were awarded their "wings" in the form of the coveted rating badge, worn on the left sleeve of their uniform. The right sleeve was reserved for rank insignia. For naval airmen this rating badge consisted of a stylized pair of wings superimposed on an anchor with a five-petaled cherry blossom above, all

Gunnery was an important part of advanced training for both pilots and observers. Here a gunner takes aim at a drogue chute from atop a Type 90 Operations Trainer (K3M).

on a circular felt patch. The colors were red on a dark blue background for winter, dark blue on white for summer. From April 1942 the colors were changed to yellow on a black background for both winter and summer uniforms.

Although they had received their "wings" the *Hiren* graduates were not yet considered fully fledged pilots. Divided now among fighter, dive bomber, torpedo bomber and other mission role assignments, the young pilots entered advanced training, or "extended education" (*encho kyoiku*) as it was known in the IJN, on operational aircraft. This final phase of pilot training lasted five or six months depending on mission role. In the prewar and China War years, *kansen* (carrier fighter) pilots received their extended education at Saeki or Oita *Kokutai*; *Kanbaku* (carrier bomber, i.e. dive bomber) pilots went to Tateyama *Kokutai*, and later, Usa *Kokutai*; *Kanko* (carrier attack plane, i.e. torpedo bomber) pilots were also typically assigned to Tateyama *Kokutai*. Their land-based counterparts, the multi-engined *Rikko* men, went to Kisarazu *Kokutai*. The aircraft used were a progression of operational types starting with the most obsolete. In the prewar and China War years, fighter pilots started on the Type 90 *Kansen*, both single-seat (A2N) and two-seat (A3N1) versions, then worked up to the Type 95 (A4N). Dive bomber pilots went from the Type 94 *Kanbaku* (D1A1) to the Type 96 (D1A2), while torpedo bomber men flew

A trainee takes aim with a flexibly mounted gun camera at a Type 96 Carrier Fighter (A5M). This was a practice exercise for the fighter pilot as well. The IJN used gun cameras in training, but not in combat.

Type 89 (B2M) and Type 92 *Kanko* (B3Y1), then continued on to the Type 96 (B4Y1).

At long last, with the end of extended education came the posting to a first-line unit. During the one-year period from the start of the *Hiren* program to the end of their extended education, enlisted pilots logged an average of 200 hours in the air. The practice of awarding "wing" patches to the pilots upon successful completion of intermediate training continued until 1940. From 1941 onwards, starting with *Sohren* Class 54, *Ko Yokaren* Class 3 and *Otsu Yokaren* Class 9, the *Hiren* program itself was extended to cover advanced training, and "wings" were awarded only at the end of the entire process. Also during the course of 1941 the entire *Hiren* program, from basic to advanced, was shortened to an average of ten months. This time frame for flight training was then maintained throughout 1942 and 1943. In 1944, however, flight training was drastically curtailed to as little as six months for many classes.

CARRIER QUALIFICATION

The Imperial Japanese Naval Air Service began life as a force of seaplanes and added carrier-based aviation soon after. During the 1930s, however, it came to include an ever-growing land-based component within its ranks. While efforts were made to give all IJN pilots some experience in carrier operations during the prewar and China War days, this became impracticable as pilot training was greatly expanded. Consequently, during the Pacific War, not all IJN airmen were carrier qualified. In fact, only the best and most well trained were selected for carrier duty, and these "airmen of the fleet" came to be looked on as the elite of the service.

In prewar days only veteran pilots with 500 hours or more of flight time were assigned to aircraft carriers and given intensive training in carrier operations for the first time at that point. But this program was accelerated with the outbreak of the war in China. In 1938, for the first time, pilots who had recently graduated from extended education with a little over 200 hours of flight time were assigned directly to aircraft carriers. The actual training process, however, remained thorough and methodical. Training in carrier landings began with landings on the ground within a restricted space of about 20m in width and 50m in length, marked out by white canvas markers simulating the dimensions of a carrier flight deck. This progressed to approaches at low altitude and speed on an actual carrier, then zooming along the flight deck at an altitude of approximately 5m without actually touching down. When the pilot had mastered the proper angle and rate of descent, he was allowed to do "touch and gos" along a clear flight deck in which he would gun his engine into a take-off immediately after his undercarriage touched down on the deck. It was only after successful completion of this process that he would be allowed to attempt a full carrier landing with the arrestor hook down. Meanwhile, the flight officer

Training for carrier landings first began with landings within a restricted space marked off on the ground with canvas strips to simulate the narrow dimensions of a carrier flight deck.

and flight deck crew kept a watchful eye, making sure that the arresting wires were up and the crash barrier raised forward. Should the need arise, the flight officer would be ready to give the pilot a wave off with a red flag, aborting his landing attempt.

Unlike carrier operations in the US and British Royal navies, the IJN did not employ landing signals officers (LSO) to stand on the flight deck and manually guide planes down. In the Imperial Navy a system of lights near the stern of the flight deck allowed pilots to guide themselves in for a landing. There were two separate rows of lights extending out from the side of the flight deck positioned at different heights, one red, the other blue. The object was for the pilot to keep the two rows perfectly aligned with each other. This allowed his aircraft to descend at the proper five- to six-degree angle for a successful touch down. If the row of red lights appeared higher to the pilot than the row of blue lights, his approach was too low. Conversely, if the red lights were seen below the blue lights, he was too high. This system was also used for guiding pilots in for night landings at airfields.

The level of flying skill among the carrier pilots of the IJN remained high during the Pacific War throughout most of 1943. Thereafter it fell off markedly as attrition among seasoned veterans and the effects of shortened training programs took their toll. By spring 1944, when the carrier fleet entered training in preparation for what became the battle of the Philippine Sea that summer, pilots were being introduced to actual flight deck landings with barely 150 hours of total flight time behind them. Training accidents, including fatalities, were numerous.

BELIEF AND BELONGING

> *"... duty is weightier than a mountain, while death is lighter than a feather."*

So reads this most famous line from the first precept of the Imperial Rescript to Japanese Soldiers and Sailors promulgated by the Emperor Meiji on January 4 1882. This rescript reflects the efforts of a nation to instil in its fighting men a strong sense of martial values as it emerged from a feudal past and aspired to greatness in an imperial world. It established a code of conduct that emphasized unquestioning loyalty,

A Type 97 Carrier Attack Plane (B5N) practices "touch and go" on the big fleet carrier *Shokaku*.

discipline, valor, honor, and frugality to the emperor. Drawing on many strands from the nation's traditions, such as Confucianism and latter-day notions of samurai virtue, it wove the fabric of a new warrior ethos that inspired many to incredible feats of courage, self-sacrifice, and devotion to duty. This *bushido* (the "way of the warrior") formed the philosophical bedrock on which stood the armed forces of imperial Japan.

The quality and strength of the Imperial Japanese Naval Air Service at its zenith owed much to this martial spirit drilled into its fighting men. Taught from childhood that Japan had never lost a war against a foreign enemy and that its shores were blessed by the divine protection of the gods, these men fought with absolute conviction in final victory. Later on, as they fought against overwhelming odds, and even in their bleakest moments, the vast majority among the rank and file believed implicitly in their ultimate triumph. They also took comfort in the sure knowledge that any who fell in battle along the way would be assured eternal rest and honour at Yasukuni Shrine, the official Shinto shrine for the nation's war dead.

To all this, however, there was a dark side. *Bushido,* so often hailed as the embodiment of the samurai spirit, was largely a myth. Essentially a creation of modern times, it was based on thoughts and writings from the latter part of the feudal era in which the warrior class was concerned with justifying its existence in a society at peace. Having little to do with the realities of samurai conduct during the preceding centuries of civil war, it projected an idealized vision of samurai virtues, emphasizing unswerving loyalty to one's lord and glorifying sacrificial death. In the context of the imperial armed forces, to die for the emperor was considered the ultimate virtue, and death in battle was a constant theme underlying the life of Japan's fighting men.

Further aggravating this preoccupation with death was the strict prohibition against capture by the enemy that came to be firmly established during the years of the China War and was formalized in the *Senjinkun* (Instructions for the Battlefield) of January 1941. Reluctance to adopt self-sealing fuel tanks and cockpit armor plate on aircraft may be attributed, in part, to the *bushido* code. Genuine acts of *jibaku* (self-destruction) by men in heavily damaged aircraft over enemy territory, and the refusal by many airmen to wear parachutes on combat missions were clear manifestations of this philosophy. Many who instinctively bailed out from burning aircraft near enemy positions subsequently released their parachute harness voluntarily and plunged to their deaths rather than face the ignominy of capture. And thus, when the time finally came, the psychological underpinnings of the suicide sorties of the Special Attack Corps were to be found already firmly in place.

Many were unyielding in their belief that these spiritual qualities and the willingness to sacrifice oneself imbued Japan's fighting men with unique strength and allowed them to prevail over an enemy with greater material resources and manpower. But ultimately, in a modern war against a numerically and technologically superior foe, the tenets of *bushido* proved anachronistic and self-defeating, particularly when the foe clung so tenaciously to life and the chance to fight again another day.

***Yokaren* trainees limber up before starting *kendo* practice. The association of the imperial armed forces with notions of medieval samurai virtue was a major part of the education and training of Japan's fighting men during the nation's imperial era. (via Edward M. Young)**

It would be wrong, however, to think that the IJN airman spent his days brooding about death, or that he was an unthinking automaton, blindly following orders. The stereotype of the Japanese airman so widely accepted in the West during the Pacific War and in the immediate postwar years stems both from Allied wartime propaganda as well as impressions gained in encounters with the poorly trained and inexperienced breed of Japanese aircrew so prevalent during 1944 and 1945. The typical airman of the IJN who had enjoyed the full prewar or early wartime program of training was a skilled and resourceful person who was quick to take the initiative. Many were colorful individuals who lived life to the full. If anything, the brutal discipline and strict regimentation of their early cadet years forged enduring bonds among classmates and, as it was designed to do, built *esprit de corps* within each group and fostered vigorous competition between groups.

Again, however, this also had its negative side. The Japanese as a people tend to form strong in-group loyalties, but this often leads to factionalism and a lack of close cooperation with those outside one's group. At the highest level the lack of cooperation between the Imperial Army and Navy was legendary in its proportions. At a lower level there were aspects of this within the IJN airmen programs, and it was aggravated further by the Japanese tendency overly to categorize the structure of their organizations. This was clearly reflected in the plethora of airmen programs established within the IJN, each with its own requirements and objectives.

The original *Yokaren,* who had prided themselves on the heritage of their program, felt superseded and relegated to "secondary" (i.e. *otsu*) status when the *Ko Yokaren* program was instituted. Furthermore, the *Ko Yokaren* enjoyed a significantly faster rate of promotion than did the *Otsu Yokaren,* and, with a year and a half lead in their level of education at the time of recruitment, some *Ko Yokaren* tended to look down on the *Otsu* boys. Friction between the two groups mounted and eventually led to a serious outbreak of violence between *Ko Yokaren* Class 8 and *Otsu Yokaren* Class 14. This led to physical separation of the two programs in March 1943 with *Ko Yokaren* remaining at Tsuchiura and *Otsu Yokaren* being transferred to Mie *Kokutai.*

As for the *Sohren,* the members of this oldest of non-commissioned airmen programs in the IJN were outraged when they found themselves redesignated as *Hei Yokaren,* which, in their minds, implied "third class".

Finally, there is no denying the gulf that existed between the officer corps on the one hand and the non-commissioned and enlisted ranks of the Imperial Navy, as a group, on the other. There were always individual examples of officers with fine leadership qualities who kept the best interests of their men at heart. These officers were remembered with genuine respect and affection by the men who served under their command. In a broader, institutional sense, however, the elitist attitudes of the graduates of the naval academy at Eta Jima towards all others, including reserve officers and "special duty" officers who had come up through the ranks, raised an impenetrable barrier against entry into the higher echelons of the naval fraternity. It is an unfortunate fact that many non-commissioned veterans of the IJN still harbor feelings of some bitterness and resentment towards their officers whom they recall as being arrogant and aloof as a class.

Ultimately, all ranks were dedicated in their service to emperor and nation, and united in their common cause against the enemy. But it is also true that the hierarchy and factionalism ever present in Japanese society had its manifestations within the IJN as well.

"Belief" and "belonging" were one and the same for the fighting men of imperial Japan and were unquestioned pillars of existence for most. But the years since 1945 have dramatically changed their world and brought new perspectives. For many veterans of the imperial armed forces, the harsh light of history and the passage of time have forced a reassessment of belief in the cause for which they had fought so fervently more than half a century ago. Others still believe. But for them all, regardless of their beliefs, their sense of comradeship and belonging are forever defined by the bonds of shared experience among "mates". In the final reckoning, the roots and branches that bind *doh-ki no sakura* – those "cherry blossoms of the same class" – one to another, are the strongest ties of all.

SPIRIT OF THE IMPERIAL JAPANESE NAVAL AIRMAN

Kisama to ore to wa	You and I are
Doh-ki no Sakura	Cherry Blossoms of the Same Class
Onaji Yokaren no	In the same garden of the Yokaren
Niwa ni Saku	We bloom

These are the opening lines of *Doh-ki no Sakura* ("Cherry Blossoms of the Same Class"), a popular song sung by thousands of enlisted airmen of the Imperial Japanese Navy during World War II.

These words encapsulate the brotherly bond forged in training and battle among the ranks of the *Hiko Yoka Renshu Sei* (Flight Reserve Trainee) Program or *Yokaren*, and highlight aspects of thought and behavior prominent among the Japanese. In a rigidly hierarchical society in which one may dominate those below but in which one is, in turn, dominated by those above, the cherished camaraderie found only among one's peers – that narrow band of brethren that one can embrace unreservedly on equal terms – looms large in the Japanese psyche.

Thus, to this day, far more than other nationalities, the Japanese identify strongly with their graduating class at school or their entry class at the company for which they work. For the ageing non-commissioned veterans of the Imperial Japanese Naval Air Service, memories of duty in China and the Pacific revolve much more closely around their comrades from the same training class than the units to which they were assigned or the ships aboard which they served.

The cherry blossom is a metaphor for the flowering of youth: beautiful yet brief, destined to be scattered by the winds of war, pledged to fall in the emperor's name. It is also a reference to the Imperial Navy itself which used the cherry blossom as insignia, in contrast to the five-pointed star of the Imperial Army.

Naval trainee pilots under inspection from senior officers of the training command. The kapok-filled life jackets were a trade mark of the IJN airman in World War II. (via Edward M. Young)

Like many Japanese songs the words are poignant and fatalistic in mood, unlike martial tunes in the West, which often convey an air of exuberance. Above all, the words resonate with sentiments universal to warriors of all ages and nations: of the unspoken loyalty among men who have trained together, messed together, fought together and who ultimately would gladly give their lives for each other.

DRESS AND APPEARANCE

For most of their history, apart from their rating insignia as aviators, the airmen of the Imperial Japanese Navy wore uniforms identical to those of other branches of the service. Thus *Yokaren* cadets wore the same open-collar shirts and caps as other enlisted seamen of the IJN, while non-commissioned and warrant officers wore the five-buttoned, high-collar jacket and peaked cap appropriate to their rank. Commissioned officers were similarly attired according to their commissioned status. The one significant exception to this pattern was instituted in November 1942 when the decision was made to change the traditional sailors' uniform of the *Yokaren* to a smart-looking, short-tunic jacket with high collar, fastened in front by seven brass buttons and accompanied by a peaked cap. These new uniforms arrived in the spring of 1943. Thereafter the seven-buttoned tunic became the distinguishing mark of the *Yokaren*.

In terms of flight clothing, all IJN airmen, regardless of rank, wore a one-piece dark brown gabardine flight suit with a large breast pocket located on the left side of the chest, as well as pockets on both trouser legs. A fur-lined collar of rabbit fur was often worn in winter. In summer a two-piece flight suit with the jacket buttoned in front was used. A silk scarf, usually white, was popular with many airmen, although other colors were also seen on occasion. A leather helmet, fur-lined in winter, was used for head covering. Leather flight gauntlets and short leather boots with rubber heels completed the outfit.

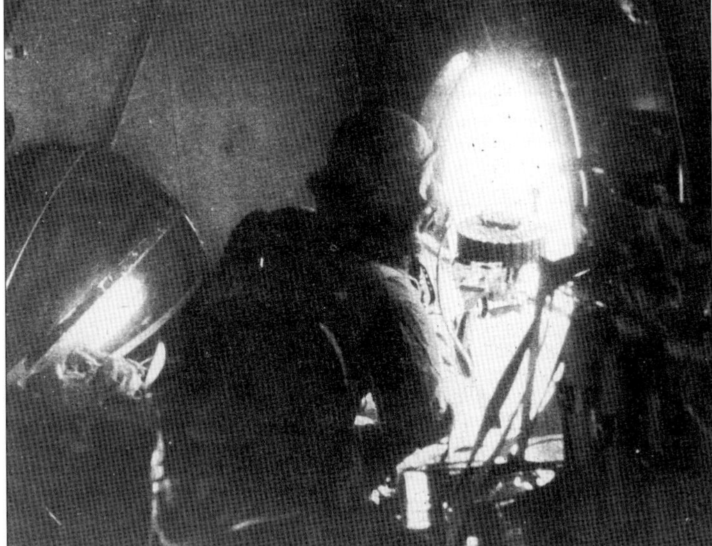

The standard hand-held aerial machine gun of the IJN Air Service for much of the 1937–45 period was the Type 92 MG. By the beginning of the Pacific War, this weapon proved woefully inadequate as a defensive armament, but continued to equip IJN aircraft for much of the conflict. (via Edward M. Young)

Beneath it all the undergarment for the IJN airman, along with his comrades in other branches of the service regardless of rank, was the loin cloth, a distinguishing feature of clothing for all men of the Imperial Navy, elegant in its simplicity. Unlike briefs, the loin cloth consisted of a bolt of cotton with a length of cotton string attached at one end, the string being tied around the waist from the back and tied in front to act as belt and support for the cloth which was wrapped over the crotch from behind and below to cover one's "vital parts".

One other feature of IJN airman appearance merits attention. All ranks in the imperial armed forces, from the lowliest army private or navy seaman to the highest-ranking general or admiral, shaved their heads. The one exception was the IJN airman. As cadets and junior enlisted aircrew, their heads were typically shaved, but as they moved up to petty officer rank they were allowed to grow their hair as additional protection for the head. Commissioned officer airmen were always allowed to grow their hair if they so chose. This was in contrast to airmen of the Imperial Army who always shaved their heads, regardless of rank.

WEAPONS AND EQUIPMENT

Armament

During the China War and the first half of the Pacific War, aircraft of the IJN were equipped primarily with 7.7mm weapons. The 7.7mm Type 97 Machine Gun, derived from a British Vickers design, was the standard fixed machine gun on IJN fighters, while the 7.7mm Type 92 Machine Gun, derived from a Lewis design, was the standard hand-held flexible weapon on multi-place aircraft. In 1937, having recognized the need for larger-caliber weapons, the IJN licensed a 20mm cannon design from the Swiss arms manufacturer Oerlikon and produced it as the Type 99 Machine Gun, both as a fixed-mounted weapon and as a hand-held, flexibly mounted version. The fixed-mounted gun was first used operationally as wing armament on the Type 0 Carrier Fighter, the world famous *Rei-sen* or "Zero" (A6M), while the hand-held version was mounted as rear-facing armament on the Type 96 Land-based Attack Aircraft (G3M) and the Type 1 Land-based Attack Aircraft (G4M). The Type 99 progressed through several versions, from the original short-barreled, drum-fed Mark 1 to the longer-barreled Mark 2 with higher muzzle velocity and range, and which was belt-fed in its later models.

It should be noted that the IJN referred to all calibers up to and including 20mm as *kikan-ju* or "machine gun", whereas the Imperial Army referred to all calibers below 12.7mm as *kikan-ju*, and calibers of 12.7mm and higher as *kikan-ho* or "machine cannon".

As an improvement on the 7.7mm Type 92, the 7.92mm Type 1 Machine Gun, based on the German Rheinmetall MG 15, was officially adopted as a hand-held weapon in March 1941 and equipped the rear cockpits of some second-generation Pacific War aircraft such as the *Suisei* (Comet) Carrier Bomber (D4Y). This weapon, however, still proved inadequate for defensive purposes.

IJN bomber crews were expected to help bomb up their own aircraft. Here a *Rikko* crewman lifts a 60kg bomb on his shoulders. (via Edward M. Young)

The 13.2mm Type 3 Machine Gun was a fixed-firing weapon which came to supersede the 7.7mm Type 97 as secondary armament on later generations of IJN fighters, including later models of the *Rei-sen*.

In addition, the IJN developed some weapons of larger caliber beyond 20mm, such as the 30mm Type 5. Following three years of development, this weapon was finally adopted for official use in May 1945 and was just entering service at the end of the Pacific War. It would have equipped future generations of IJN fighters then under development, such as the *Shinden* (J7W) canard configuration fighter and the *Shusui* (J8M) rocket-powered interceptor. The weapon was tested under combat conditions but did not see regular use before the war ended.

Bombs and torpedoes

During the course of its history the IJN produced a wide variety of aerial bombs. The most widely used, however, were those in the 60kg, 250kg, 500kg and 800kg category.

In keeping with the navy's primary mission of doing battle with an enemy fleet, bombs intended for use against ships were known as "ordinary bombs" in the Imperial Navy. High explosive bombs with larger charges and weaker casings were known as "land bombs" and were used against land targets and unprotected ships. The original 800kg bomb was of this category. Development was started around 1937 on a large bomb with particularly strong armor-piercing properties for use against capital ships. The end result was the 800kg armor-piercing bomb which was rushed into production in 1941 in time to prove its worth against the US Navy's Battleship Row at Pearl Harbor.

Other bombs developed and used during the Pacific War included the 30kg aerial burst phosphorus bombs for use against enemy aircraft formations and a 7.5kg rocket-propeled bomb developed for the same purpose in the later stages of the conflict.

Practice bombs included 1kg, 4kg and 10kg varieties, with the last being the most widely used. All were equipped to give off smoke upon contact.

The primary aerial torpedo used by the IJN throughout the 1937–45 period was the air-propeled Type 91. Continuously modified and improved during the 1930s and into the Pacific War period, this weapon eventually counted some nine versions. In its original and Modification 1 version, it measured 5.27m in total length and weighed 785kg. It could deliver a 150kg warhead at an effective distance of 2,000m at a top speed of 42. In the Mod. 2 version, overall length was increased to 5.47m and the warhead was increased to 205kg, bringing the total weight up to 838kg. Most significantly this version had a system of detachable wooden stabilisers attached to its fins which allowed it to run in shallow water. This was used in combat for the first time in the shallow depths of Pearl Harbor. The Mod. 3 was an improved Mod. 2 with a bigger warhead. The ultimate Type 91, the Mod. 7, measured 5.71m in length and had a 420kg warhead. Total weight had increased to 1,055kg. It could still run at 42 knots but effective range was reduced to 1,500m. This version, being too heavy for carrier attack aircraft, was intended exclusively for use by land-based attack planes. Later versions of the basic Type 91 design developed towards the end of the Pacific War were known as the Type 4.

The Type 94 was an oxygen-propeled torpedo for aerial use. Although adopted for official use, operational problems prevented its use in combat.

Wireless equipment

The preeminent position in the field of consumer electronics that Japan eventually came to enjoy in the decades following World War II presents a stark contrast to the deficiencies in electronic equipment suffered by her armed forces during the war years. During the 1930s the quality and effectiveness of Japan's airborne radio equipment was not far removed from those of Western air forces. But in the years just before the World War II, Japan failed to devote sufficient attention to the development of electronic warfare. In the scramble for scarce scientific and engineering resources, electronics suffered from a lack of priority, funding, and focus. The result was a major gap between Japan and her enemies as well as Germany. Japan's failure to recognize the importance of electronic warfare at an early stage was a major contributor to her ultimate defeat.

Heavier items of ordnance, such as these 250kg bombs, were carried on dollies. (via Edward M. Young)

During the China War and the early years of the Pacific War, the major front-line aircraft of the IJN were primarily equipped with the Type 96 generation of radio telegraph and radio telephone equipment. Large aircraft such as the Type 96 (G3M "Nell") and the Type 1 (G4M "Betty") Land-based Attack Aircraft and the Type 97 (H5K "Mavis") and Type 2 (H6K "Emily") Flying Boat carried both the Type 96 Air Mark 3 and Type 96 Air Mark 4 Wireless Telegraph as well as the Type 98 Air Mark 4 In-unit Radio Telephone. Two-seat aircraft such as the Type 99 (D3A "Val") and *"Suisei"* (D4Y "Judy") Carrier Bomber were equipped with the Type 96 Air Mark 2 Wireless Telegraph which had an output of 40 watts and an effective range of over 500 nautical miles. Three-seaters such as the Type 97 (B5N "Kate") and *Tenzan* (B6N "Jill") Carrier Attack Aircraft and the Type 0 Reconnaissance Seaplane (E13A "Jake") carried the Type 96 Air Mark 3 Wireless Telegraph and the Type 1 Air Mark 3 In-unit Radio Telephone. The Type 96 Air Mark 3 had an output of 50 watts and an effective range of over 800 nautical miles. It was a reliable instrument and was used effectively for many years. On many aircraft it was eventually replaced by the Type 2 Air Mark 3 Wireless Telegraph which had 80 watts of power and a range of 1,500 nautical miles. Single-seat fighters such as the Type 96 (A5M "Claude") and Type 0 (A6M "Zeke") Carrier Fighters had the Type 96 Air Mark 1 Radio Telephone, but this device suffered particularly from poor manufacture and installation as well as poor field maintenance and was practically useless in actual operations. Many of these sets were removed by front-line units to save weight. From the middle of the Pacific War, the standard fighter radio became the Type 3 Air Mark 1 Radio Telephone. With an output of 15 watts and a range of about 50 nautical miles it was an improvement on the Type 96 Mark 1, but performance still fell short of that achieved by Allied fighter short-wave radios.

DAILY LIFE AND FRONT-LINE DUTY

Posting to an operational unit or aircraft carrier of the Imperial Navy was a culture shock to many newly fledged airmen. They had endured the iron discipline and brutal beatings of their cadet years and continued to persevere under fairly strict regimentation during flight training. They were now ready to take on what they felt must surely be the even greater challenges of life in a combat unit. Imagine their surprise, therefore, to find the atmosphere quite relaxed. In some outfits the discipline was positively lax. It was sometime before they came to realize that their superiors would not berate them for every little infraction of the rules and they cautiously began to let down their guard. Many now began to sport silk scarves under their flight suits, an indulgence in fashion not allowed them during flight training and extended education. As newly promoted petty officers, there were now hardly any situations in which they would be subject to disciplinary beatings.

Pilots gather around the blackboard showing the mission-roster assignment for the day. Note the parachutes piled up on carts and the harness belts hung on the rack on the right.

Training units often had at least one advanced aircraft assigned for purposes of transition to operational duty for the pilots. Here a brand-new Type 96 Carrier Fighter sits on the edge of the runway next to rows of Type 93 Intermediate Trainers.

The training schedule in a combat unit, however, was grueling. Weather permitting, weekday mornings and afternoons were spent constantly in the air, honing air combat skills, bombing accuracy, gunnery, formation flying, and navigation. Prowess in night action was a hallowed tradition in the Imperial Navy, and as an extension of the fleet the IJN air service began to train regularly in nocturnal operations by the latter half of the 1930s. Consequently evenings were often spent in the air, practising attack and landing procedures into the late hours.

The senior pilot gives instructions on the finer points of the 96 *Kansen* to a group of pilots newly graduated from flight training.

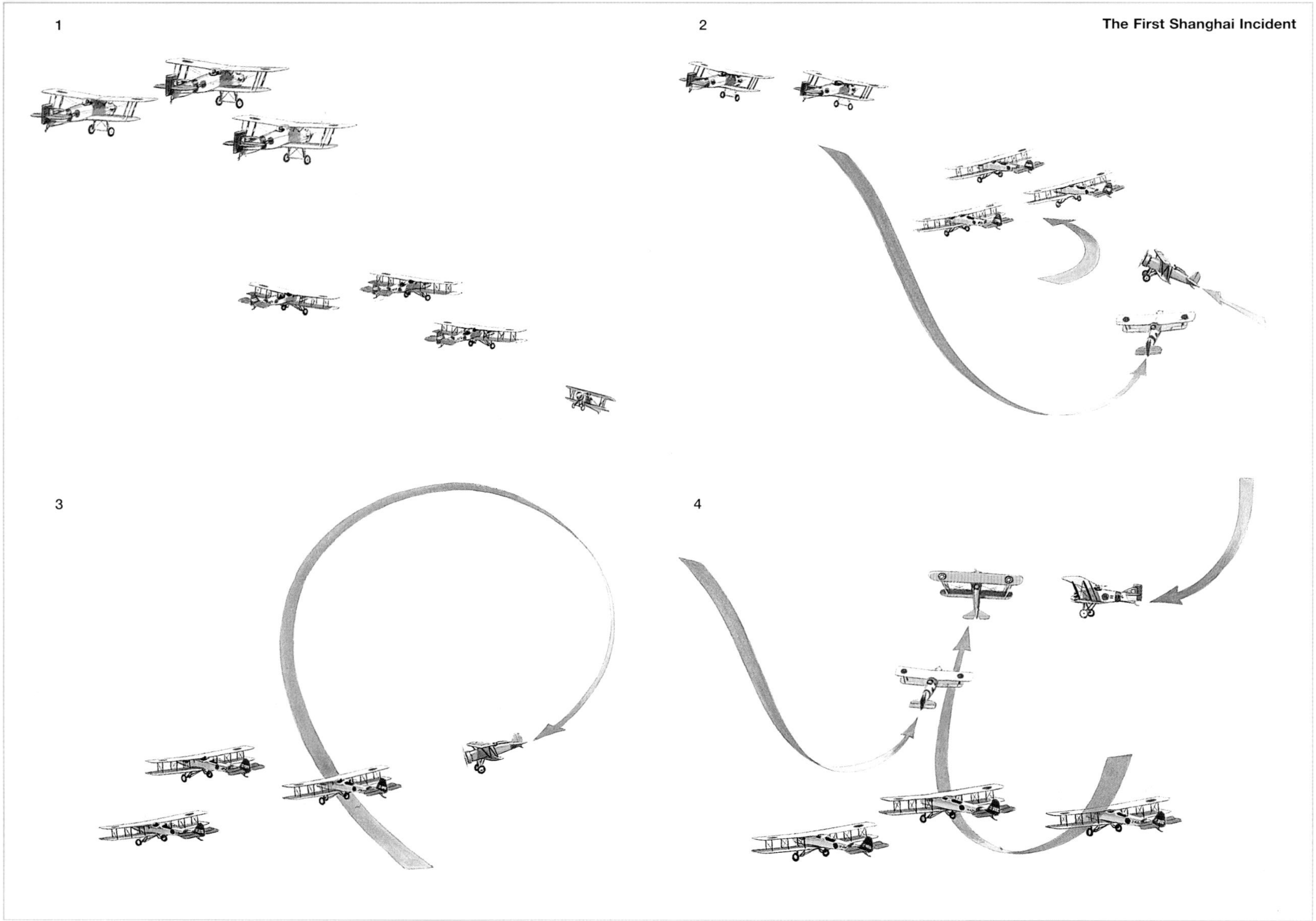

The First Shanghai Incident

1

2

3

4

A

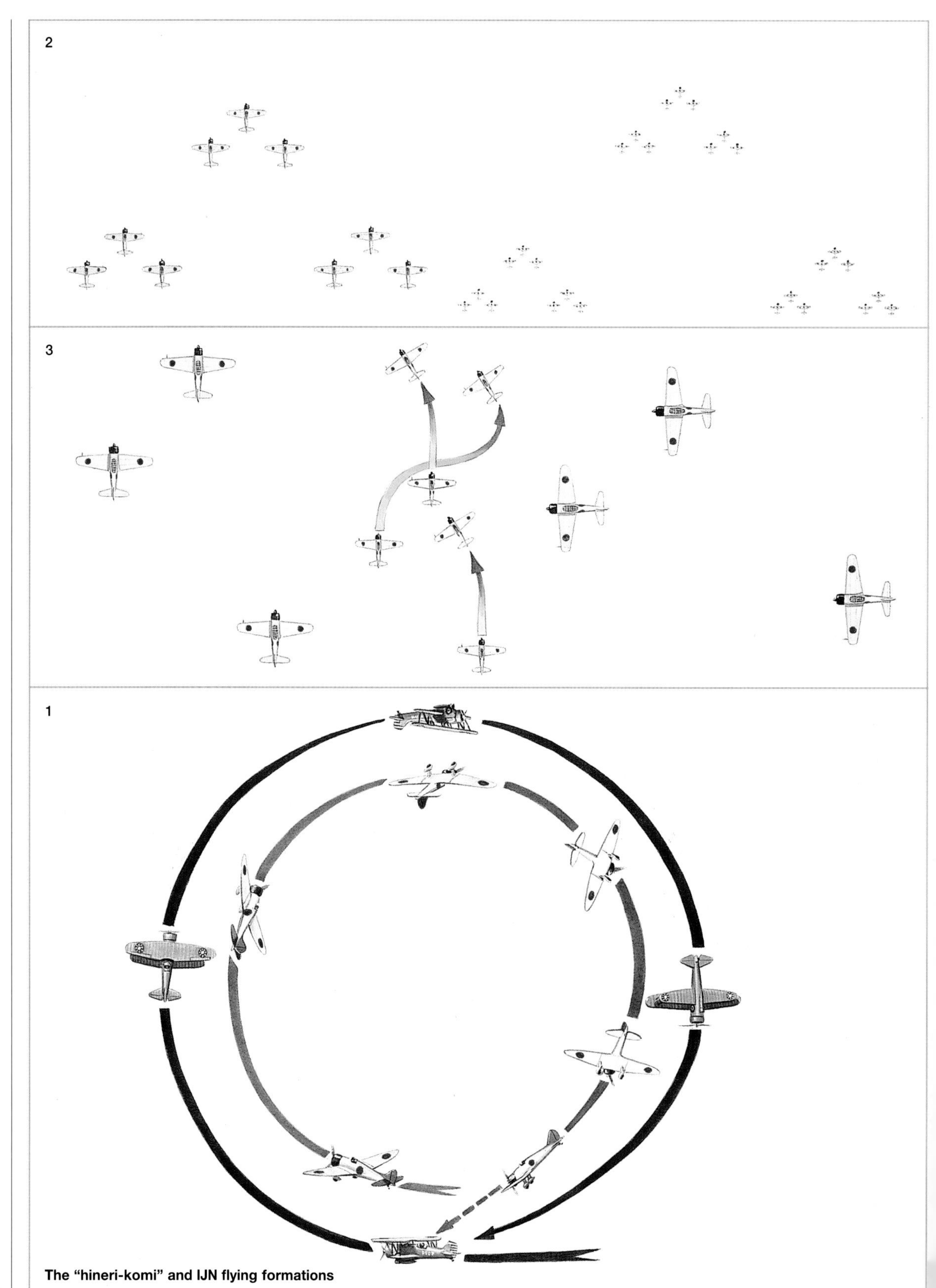

The "hineri-komi" and IJN flying formations

B

C

Standard *Rikko* Formations circa 1937–??

1

2

3

3a

3b

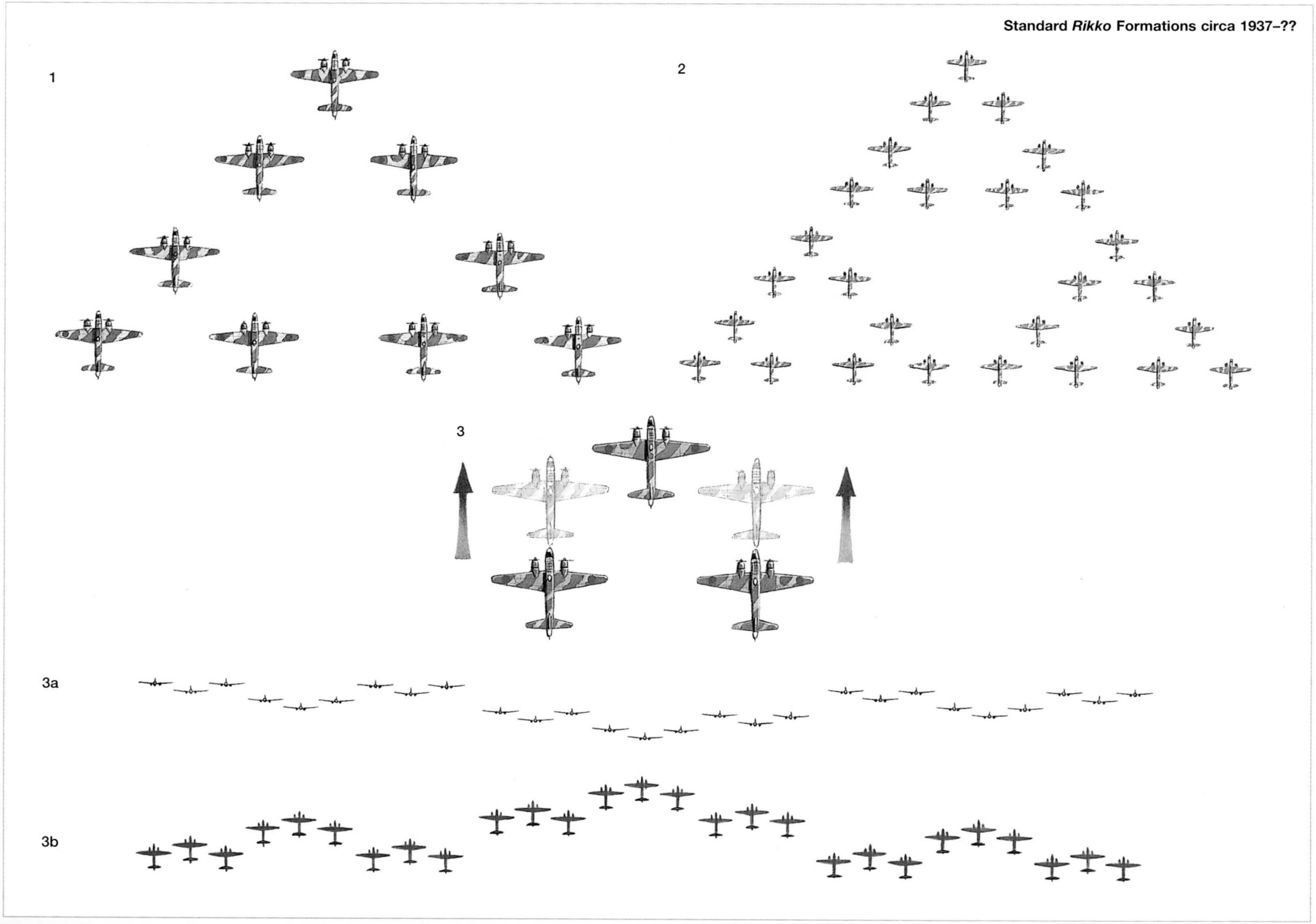

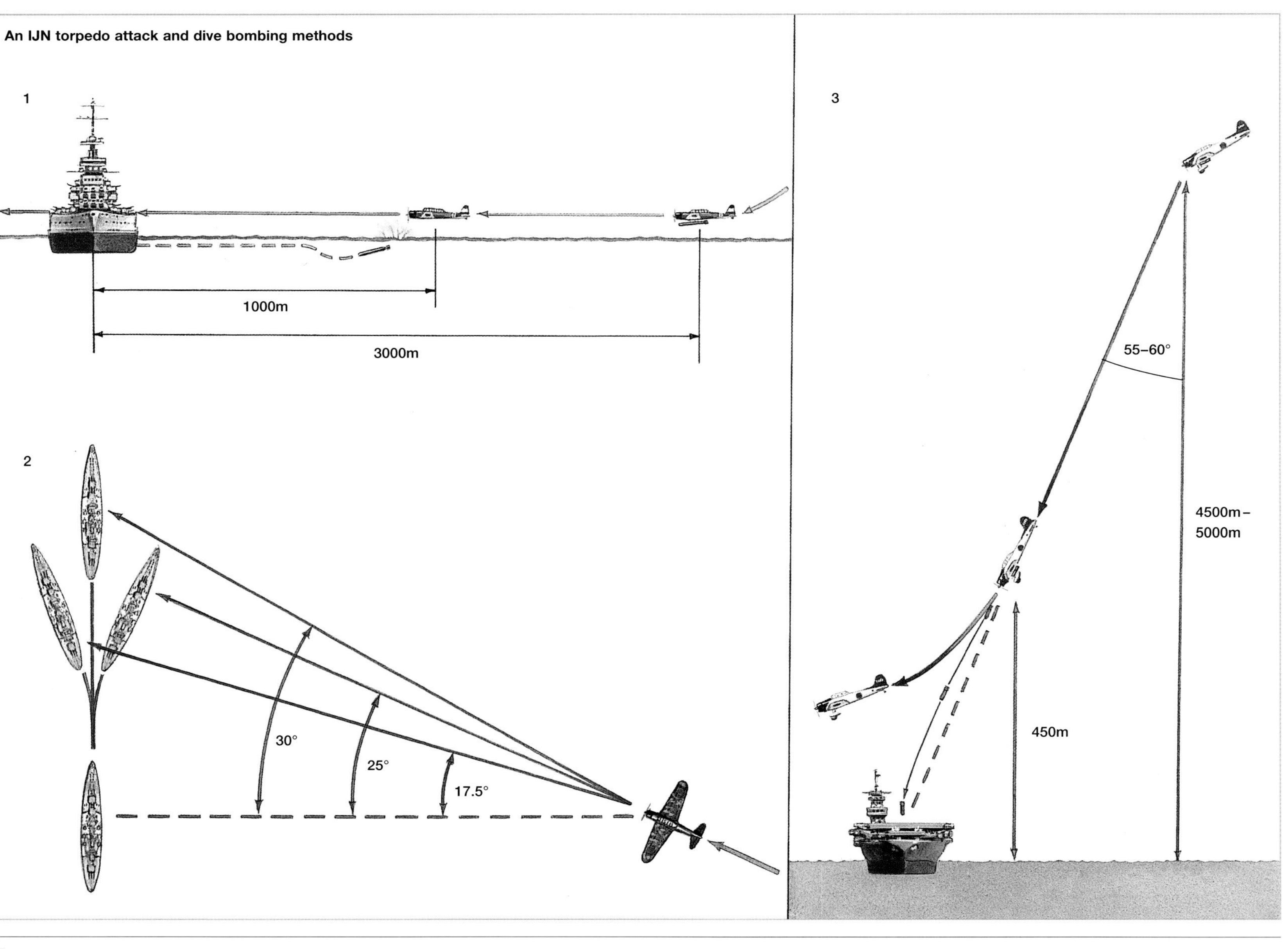

An IJN torpedo attack and dive bombing methods
1
1000m
3000m
2
30°
25°
17.5°
3
55–60°
4500m–
5000m
450m

E

Inside a Type 1 Land-based Attack Aircraft (G4M1) on operations during the Pacific War

1

2

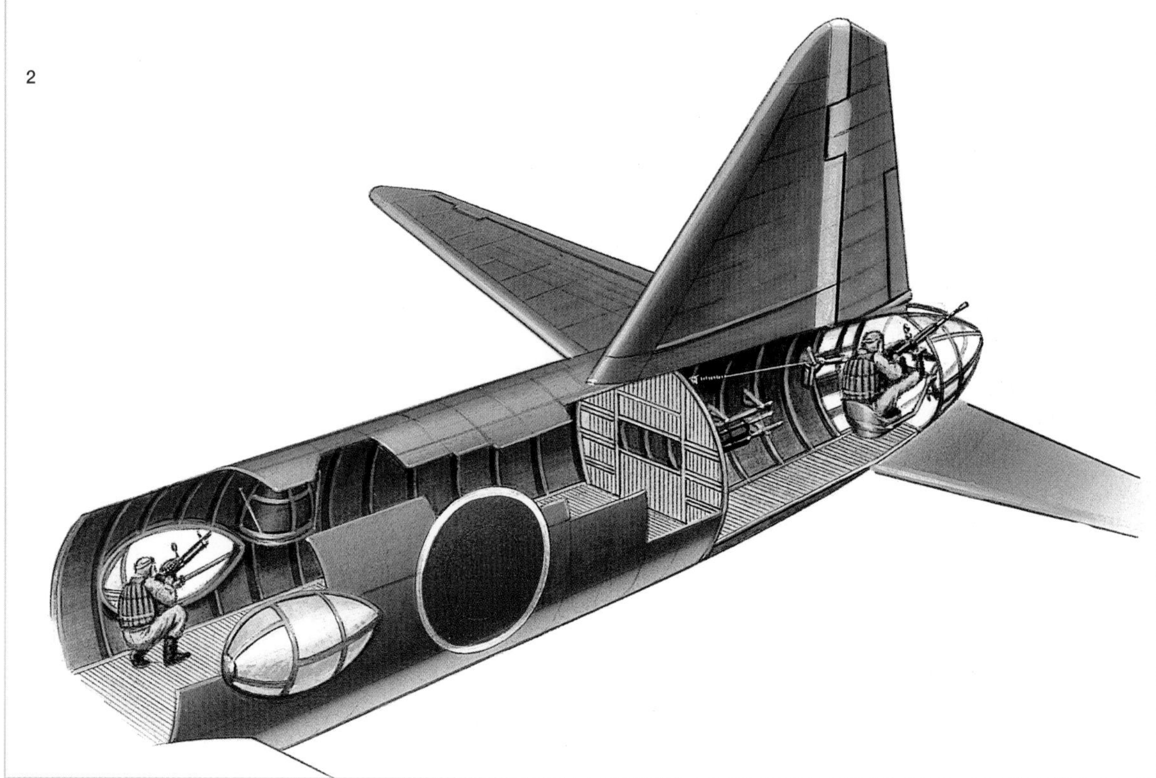

F

Rabaul

G

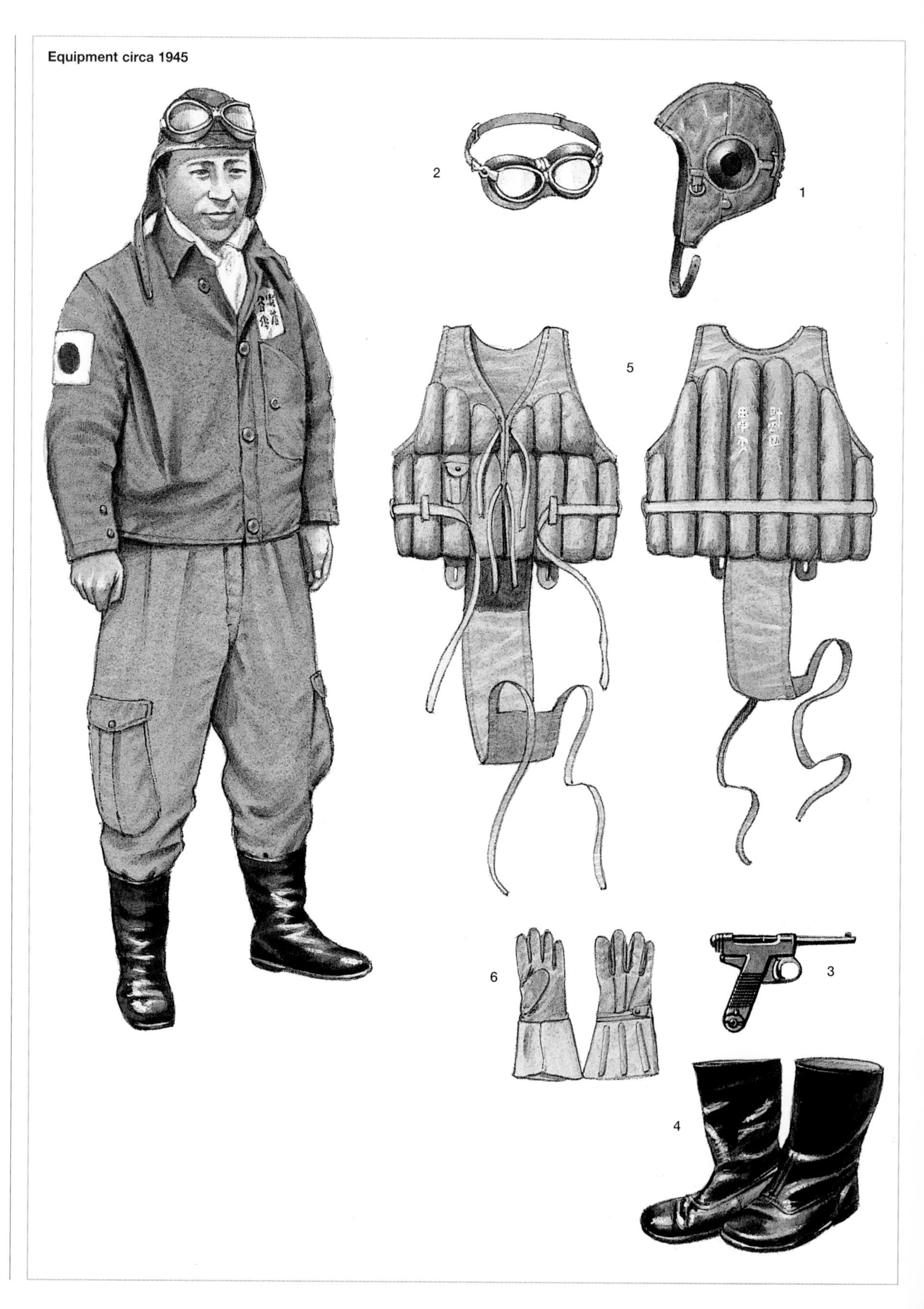
Equipment circa 1945
2
1
5
6
3
4
H

A line-up of Type 96 *Kansen* at a presentation ceremony during the China War. The Type 96 was the primary fighter of the IJN during the China conflict from 1937 until 1940 when its successor, the *Rei-sen*, made its combat debut. (via Edward M. Young)

It became apparent to the newly arrived airmen that in a first-line unit of the IJN air service, improving and maintaining operational efficiency was the be all and end all of their existence. To this everyone from the CO on down were totally dedicated, and no relaxation of standards or careless behavior was tolerated. Beyond their total commitment to flying, however, the men were generally left to their own devices. There were no martinets looking for technical infractions as an excuse to discipline the men as, all too often, there had been in the past. "Eat, drink and live life to the full" was the attitude, and "for tomorrow, you shall willingly give your life for the Emperor" was the implicit understanding.

Most units maintained rented accommodations in the local town for use by their men during "shore leave". No longer minors, many airmen now acquired a taste for *sake* and women. Weekends spent in movie houses and cheap restaurants, then adjourning later to places serving liquor were to provide fond memories for many IJN airmen. Monday mornings would often be spent sitting in deck-chairs along the flight line, pretending to watch squadron mates practice take-offs and landings, while sunglasses concealed closed eyelids sleeping off the hangover from the night before.

Lavish parties at exclusive restaurants with proper *geisha* in attendance were reserved for special occasions such as the culmination of a major fleet exercise. Officers would invariably pick up the tab at such events. On their own, those petty officers who were inclined to do so were generally content to consort with the less refined sisters of the entertainment sorority in the less reputable establishments of the local town.

Pilots report back after a mission in China, as senior officers listen to the leader's report. Note the rope lanyards over the backs of the men in the foreground. These held Nambu pistols in place on the front of their life jackets. (via Edward M. Young)

A Type 96 Carrier Bomber (D1A2) in flight. The dive bomber pilots of the IJN flew this aircraft either during "extended education" training or on operations in China. It was the mainstay of the IJN dive bomber force before the advent of the Type 99 (D3A). (via Edward M. Young)

During the China War years airmen would typically be assigned to duty on the continent following an initial posting of about six months in a first-line unit in Japan or a ship of the fleet. This allowed opportunities for combat to be given to a large number of airmen. For bomber crews, duty in China brought considerable action as well as hazard throughout much of the IJN's participation in that conflict. In 1937, during its initial phase, *kanko* (carrier attack), *kanbaku* (carrier bomber) and *Rikko* (land attack) planes all suffered heavy casualties. Later, during long-range penetration missions to targets such as Chungking, Chengtu, and Lanchow, the *Rikko* crews sustained significant casualties once more. Flown without the benefit of fighter escort, these missions often met stiff opposition from the remnants of the Chinese Nationalist Air Force still defending the last bastions of unoccupied China deep in the interior.

For the fighter pilots of the IJN, China brought sustained air combat on a large scale for the first time and gave rise to their first "Aces". The Japanese never subscribed to the formal definition of an "Ace" as applied in the West, namely a pilot who had shot down at least five enemy aircraft. Official policy in the Japanese air forces always emphasized teamwork and discouraged individual "stardom". But everyone naturally recognized those who had achieved an outstanding record of downing enemy aircraft. These men came to be known as *gekitsui-oh* (literally "shoot-down king"). Although never clearly defined, an airman usually required some seven to ten victories in order to receive that accolade. But after the fall of Nanking in December 1937 and the flurry of air activity over Hankow during the summer of 1938 leading up to its capture in October of that year, the IJN fighter force had little to do. The introduction of the Zero in the summer of 1940 finally gave the fighter pilots sufficient range to reach the last remaining enclaves of Chinese fighters, but until then, the Type 96 *Kansen* (A5M "Claude")-equipped fighter force could contribute little more than routine air patrols over their bases and participation in occasional ground support missions. The two-year period from the summer of 1938 to the summer of 1940, therefore, was a time of limited opportunity for the fighter pilots of the IJN.

The war in China was a strange experience in many ways. There was a limit to the amount of territory that Japanese troops could occupy in a country the size of China. Once they had captured most of the major cities and ports, and had control of the main rivers, the advance simply stopped. For their part, the Chinese lacked the industrial strength and logistics to mount a major counteroffensive, and their leaders, for their own complex political reasons, preferred to play a waiting game rather than pursue vigorous opposition. The Japanese merely controlled the urban centers and the thin lines of communication between them. The countryside belonged to the Chinese. In most areas there was no well-

A land-based attack aircraft crew take a meal by their aircraft before a mission. They wear life jackets, indicating an over-water mission, but no parachutes. (via Edward M. Young)

Silhouetted against the late-afternoon sky, a Type 96 returns from operations over China. The elliptical wings of the A5M were a characteristic feature of this the first operational all-metal fighter in the IJN. (via Edward M. Young)

Type 96 Land-based Attack Aircraft (G3M) in formation on a deep penetration mission over China. These long-range, unescorted missions by the *Rikko* resulted in some heavy losses to Chinese fighters until the appearance of the Type 0 Carrier Fighter (A6M). (via Edward M. Young)

defined front line and the local Chinese population moved freely between the countryside and the towns. Local commerce continued to flourish in many areas.

For the airmen of the IJN, duty in China was a strange mixture of life and death struggle, in short bursts, together with the relative comforts of urban life and the added spice of an exotic foreign flavor not available back home. Certain precautions were necessary, to be sure. Excursions away from the safety of the air base at night was prohibited in many places and, even in daytime, one never traveled alone if one could help it. But every major town had establishments run by resident Japanese or accommodating Chinese which offered havens of relaxation amid surroundings of questionable allegiance.

All those who experienced China for the first time were struck by the sheer vastness of the country, so different in scale from the hills and small, neatly cultivated rice paddies of home. Airmen sometimes had to contend with violent weather phenomena, born of the continental geography, which one could hardly imagine in the homeland. Similarly, the temperature extremes that one had to endure in the inland areas of China were far beyond anything in the experience of the Japanese home islands. The scorching heat of summer in Hankow was legendary. "A bird landed on telephone wires and instantly dropped dead to the ground, deep fried" was a standard joke among Japanese servicemen there. Going to high altitude on operations was a relief under those circumstances.

Following duty in China, which could range anywhere from several months to as long as a year, many IJN airmen were transferred back to Japan for a tour of duty as flight instructors in training units. Many were given several days leave upon return from the continent before starting their new assignment, and most typically took advantage of this opportunity to visit family back home.

During the course of 1941, as the Pacific War approached, the relatively routine pace of life began to change. Training schedules became intensified. Eventually they became round the clock. Saturdays and Sundays disappeared from the weekly schedule. Instead, Monday and Friday schedules were repeated twice. "Mon., Mon., Tues., Wed., Thurs., Fri., Fri." was a classic refrain in the IJN which referred to intense, round-the-clock training.

TACTICS

Fighters

On February 22 1932, during the brief First Shanghai Incident, the IJN air service achieved the first aerial victory in its history. The Japanese fighter aircraft involved in that action were flying a classic, tight "vic" formation of three aircraft derived from British RAF fighter doctrine as it existed during the interwar period.

At the start of the China War in 1937, however, the Japanese discovered that the tight "vic" lacked flexibility in actual combat and soon adopted a looser formation in which the two wingmen were spread out behind their leader. This allowed greater room for maneuver and made for quicker response time in a combat encounter. The basic tactical

A *chutai* of Type 96 *Kansen* in flight during the China War. The *shotai* in the distance appears to be one man short. (via Edward M. Young)

A formation of Type 96 *Rikko* shows the classic three-plane *shotai* formations flown by the land attack corps. (via Edward M. Young)

formation flown, however, remained a *shotai* of three planes, while the basic premise of air combat training remained that of a one-on-one dogfighting dual between two opponents. In this context, the *hineri-komi* or "twisting-in" maneuver, first developed at Yokosuka *Kokutai* during 1934, proved to be a formidable combat tool. This "corkscrew" loop maneuver allowed a pursuer to cut down his turning radius and quickly achieve an attacking position above and behind an opponent who executed a standard loop. Used often during the China War and to some extent during the early months of the Pacific War, it was this maneuver, even more than the inherent maneuvrability of the fighters they flew, that established the IJN fighter pilot as a remarkable dogfighter. While other maneuvers in their air combat repertoire, such as the snap roll, Immelmann turn and split-S, were shared with fighter pilots of all nations, the *hineri-komi* was unique to the Japanese fighter pilots of this period.

During the China War, despite training in formation discipline, aerial battles often degenerated into a wild melee of twisting and turning individuals. In the lead-up to the Pacific

War during the autumn of 1941, coordination in air combat from the *shotai* level up to *chutai* and *daitai* levels became the focus of intense training. When the Pacific War began, the IJN fighter pilot had greatly improved his skills in taking coordinated action, particularly at the *shotai* and *chutai* levels. This enhanced ability to coordinate action within larger formations, however, was possible only because the units involved were manned by experienced pilots who constantly drilled together as a team. As the Pacific War progressed and attrition took a steady toll of veteran pilots, the ability to coordinate combat action deteriorated. Suffering from a lack of radar-directed interception and effective short-wave radios in their fighters, Japanese pilots were never able to achieve the level of coordination that their opponents brought to bear on them.

Enjoying great success with their standard three-plane *shotai* formations during much of the first year of the Pacific War, the Japanese were slow to adopt the two-plane element and four-plane division formations already being used by many of the world's major air forces. Yokosuka *Kokutai* experimented with these formations during the latter half of 1942, and limited use was made of them in combat during the first half of 1943. But *rotte* tactics, as this formation was known to the Japanese who borrowed Luftwaffe terminology in reference to it, did not become established within the IJN fighter force until the latter half of 1943. It was first adopted on a regular basis by 204 *Kokutai* from the beginning of June 1943 over the Solomon Islands. Other units followed, and by the end of that year, it had replaced the three-plane *shotai* as the standard fighter formation of the IJN.

By 1944 IJN terminology for fighter formations had changed to reflect the new tactics. The two-plane element was referred to as a *hentai*. Two *hentai* made up a four-plane formation known as a *kutai*. The *shotai* now became a formation of eight aircraft, made up of two *kutai*, while a *chutai* consisted of 16 aircraft in two *shotai* of eight planes each.

On long-range missions, meals were usually taken on board. Here, the junior navigator on board a 96 *Rikko* enjoys a meal from his aluminum lunch box. The cockpit of the Type 96 was much more cramped than that of its successor, the Type 1 *Rikko* (G4M). (via Edward M. Young)

Horizontal bombers

During the interwar period most nations overestimated the defensive capabilities of the multi-engined bomber and the ability of the bomber to "always get through" in the face of enemy opposition. The Japanese were no exception. At the beginning of the China War, IJN doctrine called for their new Type 96 *Rikko* (G3M1 "Nell") to penetrate enemy air space in small formations of *shotai* (three-plane) size and to attack at medium altitude (3,000 to 5,000m). Heavy casualties at the hands of Chinese fighters in the opening phase of the war in August 1937 proved a rude awakening for the IJN. Larger formations and

The continental weather was always a challenge for the long-ranging *Rikko*, here flying through some heavy cumulus over Southeast Asia. (via Edward M. Young)

higher operating altitudes were adopted. A nine-plane *chutai* arranged in a "V of V" formation of three *shotai* of three planes each became the standard combat formation. The largest formations adopted consisted of a *daitai* of 27 aircraft in a "V of V" made up of three *chutai*. When heavy opposition was expected, the formation would go to 7,000m altitude or higher. In an effort to throw off the aim of enemy anti-aircraft (AA) defences, bombing was sometimes conducted in a shallow five degree formation dive rather than in straight and level flight.

Defense against enemy interceptors took the form of a long line-abreast formation formed by the wingmen in each *shotai*, and the wing formations in progressively larger formations, moving up almost abreast of the leader. This allowed a high concentration of defensive fire to be brought to bear on attacking fighters. The aircraft at the extreme ends of the formation, however, were most exposed and experience showed that this position suffered the greatest rate of casualty. Known in Japanese airman slang as the *kamo* position – equivalent to the English "sitting duck" – it was usually the lot of the junior-most crews to assume the position.

From the latter half of 1942 on into 1943, ever mounting casualties in the face of increasingly effective Allied defences put an end to large "V of V" formations flown on daylight missions. The emphasis switched thereafter to nocturnal missions flown at medium and low altitude by small formations and single aircraft.

The poor rate of accuracy achieved by horizontal bombing in comparison to dive bombing and torpedo attack was a vexing problem within the IJN during the interwar and China War years. The solution was a system of lead bombardiers instituted during 1940–41. All aircraft in a bombing formation dropped their bombs simultaneously on a signal from the lead aircraft, but the choice of bombardier in the lead aircraft had previously been made merely on the basis of seniority. Now, selected individuals who had shown particular aptitude in bomb aiming were given a special intensive training course on the task, and, upon return to their units, became designated as lead bombardiers.

The pairing of the bombardier with his usual pilot was also critical. Unlike the American Norden bombsight, the Type 90 and Type 92 Bombsights then in use by the IJN lacked an autopilot link between the bombardier and the lateral movement of the aircraft. Thus, the instinctive coordination between bombardier and pilot, achieved only after long hours of practice as a team, was a crucial element in bombing success. During the approach to and withdrawal from the target, a bomber formation would be led by the senior officer on the mission. If his aircraft carried the lead bombardier, no change in formation would take place. Quite often, however, the aircraft carrying the lead bombardier flew on the leader's wing, the bombardier being paired with a senior warrant officer pilot rather than the mission leader. In such cases, the mission leader's aircraft would exchange places with the lead bombardier's aeroplane during the initial approach to the target and allow the latter to lead on the actual bomb run. Such was the case at Pearl Harbor among the Type 97 *Kanko* (B5N2) Horizontal Bombers. Also at Pearl Harbor, in a departure from the usual nine-plane "V of V" formation, a special five-plane "V" formation was used by the horizontal bombers in order to achieve a higher concentration of bombs within limited airspace in attacking Battleship Row.

Torpedo bombers

The torpedo bombers of the IJN prided themselves on wielding the most effective aerial weapon in a fleet engagement. They were also resigned, in true *bushido* fashion, to the highest casualty rates.

Approaching battle in a shallow dive, the torpedo bomber would level out for its torpedo run some 3,000m from the target ship.

A happy crew return from their flight, carrying their equipment in a couple of suit cases. No life jackets are worn, indicating a mission over land. Again, no parachutes are carried – a point of honor with the *Rikko* men in combat. (via Edward M. Young)

Maintaining an altitude of 10 to 20m above the waves, the crew of the aircraft would bore into within 1,000m before releasing their torpedo. Following torpedo launch, the aircraft would continue straight on towards the target vessel, thereby presenting a smaller target to the ship's anti-aircraft gunners than it would by turning broadside in order to turn for a getaway. The object was to keep below the level of the ship's deck until the last minute, then hurdle over the vessel and continue the withdrawal on the other side, skimming the waves once more.

Prewar exercises indicated that torpedo bomber crews would have to be prepared to suffer casualty rates as high as 70 percent. Even higher loss rates became a reality in confronting the formidable defenses of the US fleet during the Pacific War. Ultimately torpedo bombing by the IJN, as with high-level, horizontal bombing, was forced to seek the cloak of night. In night torpedo attacks, the attacking force was divided into two mission roles. An illumination force flew ahead and dropped parachute flares, both to illuminate the target at night and to indicate the target's direction and speed using color-coded flares, while the strike force followed behind and attacked in the standard manner previously described for daylight attacks.

Dive bombers

Dive bombers in the IJN approached their target in a shallow dive from high altitude, and, visibility permitting, usually pushed over into their dives at an altitude of about 5,000m. The preferred diving angle was between 55 and 60 degrees. Pull out would normally be at 450m in combat, although veteran crews would often hold their dive until 300m, pulling out and leveling off just above the ground or ocean. In doing so, however, proper altimeter reading by the observer in the rear cockpit was crucial. Each complete revolution of the altimeter represented 500m of altitude. A mistake in counting the number of revolutions on the altimeter would thus have fatal consequences.

At the start of the China War, IJN *kanbaku* flew a line-astern or stepped-echelon formation, with each aircraft pushing over into its dive at nearly the same point in the air. This tended to cause high casualties as enemy gunners quickly learned to focus their fire on that point. Thereafter, the *kanbaku* reserved this method of attack for lightly defended targets. For more heavily defended targets, they adopted a method of attack in which each *shotai* of three aircraft would dive together, with various *shotai* attacking from different directions.

In the latter half of the Pacific War, as the intensity of American anti-aircraft fire made conventional dive bombing practically suicidal, the IJN adopted a simultaneous attack by a full *chutai* of aircraft diving in unison from a line-abreast formation.

THE IMPERIAL JAPANESE NAVAL AIRMAN IN COMBAT

"Somewhere in the South Pacific" was a familiar phrase in news dispatches on the Allied side during the Pacific War. The need for security cloaked references to specific place names in a blanket of anonymity and conjured up exotic images of combat on jungle-covered islands in the minds of

people back home. An equivalent literary device used by Japanese war correspondents involved news dispatches from "Base OO" on the "Southern Front".

During the fierce campaign of attrition fought in the Solomon Islands and Eastern New Guinea for nearly two years from the summer of 1942 until the spring of 1944, the opposing forces were well matched and the issue often in doubt. In the air, this period represented the longest continuous campaign of the entire Pacific War, and victories on both sides were hard earned against generally skilled opponents. Buin, on the southeastern tip of Bougainville Island, was one of the most forward of Japanese air bases for much of this period. From October 1942, when it first became operational with the IJN, until it was finally neutralized and by-passed by the advancing Allies a year later, it provided a vital base for Japan's air effort during the Guadalcanal campaign and the subsequent struggle for the Central Solomons. We shall now return to that time, more than half a century ago, and follow the experiences of a "typical" fighter pilot of the Imperial Japanese Navy, fighting against ever mounting odds from "Base OO" somewhere on the "Southern Front".

Type 0 Carrier Fighters (A6M) in the dispersal area surrounded by jungle at Buin on Bougainville. Note the Japanese-style steel matting on the ground. (USAF photograph)

A Type 0 Observation Seaplane (F1M) takes off on a mission over the Solomon Islands. Despite its obsolete biplane configuration and cumbersome floats, the F1M performed a great service for the IJN in the South Pacific.

Rising well before dawn, Flight Petty Officer 1st Class "Hattori", as we shall call our IJN pilot, finished his spartan breakfast of barley rice and *miso* soup at the mess near his quarters, a collection of tents set in the jungle at the southern end of the airfield. In the rear areas, where supplies were still relatively plentiful, care was taken to give aircrew added nutrition in the form of eggs and fresh fruit. But at forward bases such as this they had to make do with whatever supplies were available and they ate the same fare as everyone else. They counted their blessings. At least they were not reduced to a steady diet of locally grown sweet potatoes which ground personnel at satellite bases further afield were already forced to endure.

Along with others slated for the upcoming mission, Hattori hitched a ride on a Nissan truck from the base motor pool for the 4km ride to the airfield. Take-off was shortly after dawn at 0500 hrs Tokyo Time (TT). He was to lead his two wingmen, Flyer 1st Class "Sato" and Flyer 2nd Class "Kimura", as we shall call them. Together they formed the second *shotai* in a nine-plane *chutai* formation flying the first shift of the day to provide air cover over a convoy run to Guadalcanal. Japanese forces always operated on Tokyo Time, regardless of their location. 0500 hrs TT equated to 0600 hrs local time at their base.

The airfield consisted of a single, narrow runway, about 800m long and no more than 30 or 40m wide running north to south from the jungle to the sea. A width of about 10m down the center of the runway was paved with steel plates. Take-off, especially with auxiliary fuel tanks, always had to be towards the sea. The northern end of the field ended in thick jungle.

The *chutai* of Mark 1 *Rei-sen* (A6M2 Model 21) arrived over the ships at 0600 hrs (TT) near Rendova, and flew patrol at 3,000m altitude for two hours until relieved by the second shift at 0805 hrs. The planes of the relief shift approached waggling their wings to identify themselves as friendly, and the first shift responded in kind. The Type 96-1 Voice Radios in their fighters were of such poor quality as to be practically useless and nobody used them. Communication between fighters was normally limited to hand signals, wing movements or, when circumstances allowed, simple messages written on hand-held chalk boards displayed from the cockpit.

Hattori was glad to be flying an old Mitsubishi-built Mark 1. Like many veterans, he did not care much for the newer Mark 2 (A6M3 Model 32). Despite the more powerful engine and faster speed of the

The IJN came under increasing pressure from growing Allied strength as the Pacific War continued. Here, in October 1943, Rabaul comes under heavy attack by bombers of the USAAF. By this time, Buin on Bougainville had been practically neutralized. (USAF photograph)

Mark 2 he still preferred the greater maneuvrability and more finely balanced handling qualities of the Mark 1, not to mention its greater range. Furthermore, he preferred the older Mark 1s built by Mitsubishi to the newer Mark 1s licence-built by Nakajima as the latter gave less trouble with engine oil leaks, but the Mitsubishi airframes were better built in his view, an opinion shared by others in his unit.

The need to maintain vigilance and fend off boredom during convoy escort was always hard on the nerves, especially when no enemy appeared. This uneventful patrol had been a repeat of the previous day, and of a similar mission in which Hattori had participated the week before. At this stage of the war air combat did not occur on a daily basis despite the overall intensity of the campaign. Rather, brief encounters with the enemy were focal points of activity interspersed with long stretches of uneventful duty, and the days quickly blurred into each other in one's mind.

As the *chutai* headed northwest back towards base, the weather, which until then had been so clear, began to change. Soon a black curtain of cloud barred their path. Tendrils of mist drooping almost to sea level obscured the horizon and revealed torrential rains pelting the ocean below. The weather front stretched across their flight path on both sides as far as the eye could see and offered no way around it. At first the *chutai* leader tried to take the formation above the wall of cloud, but gave up after reaching 8,000m with the boiling mass of cumulus still towering above them. There was no choice but to fly through the front. They could brave the thermals inside the clouds or hug the ocean through solid sheets of rain and hope nobody would hit a wave. Through hand signals the leader ordered the *chutai* to spread out and break up into individual *shotai* in order to brave the violent air currents inside the cloud. Hattori in turn signalled Sato and Kimura to stay close and never lose sight of him under any circumstances. As they plunged into the white mass, the turbulence inside the cloud grabbed hold of the *Rei-sen* and tossed them about violently. Hattori kept his eyes glued to his instruments, with an occasional glance back at his two wingmen to make sure they were still with him. It was very easy to lose one's orientation completely under such conditions.

After what seemed an eternity they suddenly broke out into clear, calm sky and managed to reach base at 1005 hrs, some 45 minutes later than the flight would normally have taken them. But the challenges of this mission were not yet over. The tropical storm through which they had flown had previously dumped its rains on the airfield, and beyond the narrow strip of steel matting, the runway was a sea of mud. Hattori and Sato managed to land without mishap, but Kimura, the No. 3 man, ground looped just beyond the strip and broke his undercarriage. Hattori's *shotai* was the last flight to reach base, but the third *shotai*, which had preceded them, returned short of one man. Its leader and his No. 2 had returned together after having gone to low altitude and flying through zero visibility "on the deck". While doing so, however, their No. 3 had become separated. The eight men of the *chutai* waited by the airfield for as long as they could, but the missing pilot did not return. A Type 0 observation Seaplane (F1M "Pete") was sent out of Shortland to search for him but came back later in the afternoon empty handed. Airmen on both sides in the Pacific War came to learn through bitter experience that the weather could often be more deadly than the enemy.

There was little time to rest or worry about the fate of one of their men. With most of the pilots out providing air cover for the convoy in relays, every spare man was needed for other duties. Not long after his return, Hattori was ordered to fly standing patrol above the base and was told to get lunch first. He wolfed down some *onigiri* rice balls wrapped in *nori* (dried seaweed) and washed it down with tea, fighting the swarm of flies that constantly plagued the base.

Hattori was in the air again shortly after 1100 hrs with two wingmen. Sato was his No. 2 once more, but Flyer 2nd Class Hashimoto, a recent arrival, replaced Kimura as his No. 3. B-17s and B-24s, often flying alone, had been coming over almost daily on reconnaissance. They would invariably make their appearance around noon. One could almost set one's watch by the regularity of their schedule.

Predicting their appearance was one thing, but shooting them down was quite another. The American four-engined bombers boasted formidable defenses, so unlike their own vulnerable twin-engined *Rikko.* The best method of attacking them was a constant topic of discussion among the pilots. In time, through a process of trial and error, they would come to favour oblique frontal passes and vertical diving attacks from directly overhead as the most effective means of bringing down the American heavies. But perfection of these methods still lay in the future. On this day Hattori and his colleagues hoped only to find some chink in their armor which would reveal a vulnerable spot.

As they circled over their base at 5,000m altitude Hattori caught a glint of sunshine reflecting off metal out of the corner of his eye. The tiny speck soon materialized into the familiar shape of a B-17 as Hattori and his wingmen climbed to higher altitude to intercept. Lookouts on the ground had also spotted the intruder and their alarm brought up three more *Rei-sen* which had been on standby alert at the edge of the field.

Hattori approached the B-17 on a curving trajectory and opened his attack with a frontal pass, concentrating his fire on the bomber's left wing root and then diving beneath his target. His wingmen followed suit. Hattori now led his *shotai* around for a beam attack on the bomber, side slipping as he approached and straightening out just long enough to squeeze out a burst at the B-17's mid-section. As he crossed over the bomber he kicked rudder and threw his *Rei-sen* back into a skid. Glancing back he noticed Hashimoto's 'plane trailing a thin white stream of fuel from his wing. Luckily there appeared to be no fire, but Hashimoto was out of the fight. Hattori signaled him to land and reminded himself to lecture Hashimoto later. This fellow was one of the newer replacement pilots. He had yet to learn what the more seasoned pilots all understood: that in combat, flying in a straight direction or making smooth turns would lead to a fiery death, especially since the 13mm guns of the enemy had a flatter trajectory and longer effective range than their own short-barreled 20mms. Hattori and Sato made two more passes at the B-17. They could swear they saw numerous hits on the big bomber, but it stubbornly continued to fly on, seemingly unhurt.

On the last pass the two men were joined by the standby Zeros which had finally reached the scene of action after a 20-minute

Land-based attack aircraft crewmen share a quiet moment together in the pre-dawn darkness as one of them plays a haunting melody on his *shakuhachi* (Japanese flute). (via Edward M. Young)

pursuit. Hattori noticed that these newcomers to the battle were opening fire at too great a distance from their target. He now realized that the unusually large size of the four-engined bomber was causing the fighter pilots to misjudge the range, their only familiar frame of reference being the smaller, twin-engined *Rikko* of their own forces. On his final pass, Hattori bored in and held his course until the last possible moment before veering off to avoid a collision and finally managed to smoke one of the bomber's engines. At that point, however, the B-17 managed to escape into a cloud bank at 6,000m altitude. Once again, they had been unable to bring down the big American bomber.

Pilots returning from the fourth shift over the convoy brought back reports of a big battle with Grumman F4F fighters and Douglas SBD dive bombers sent out to attack the Japanese ships approaching Guadalcanal. One transport had been hit but continued on toward the island.

Everyone off duty gathered in front of the command post to hear news of the action. The command post, of wooden frame and panel construction, located midway down the west side of the airfield, was an imposing structure with its floor raised high above ground on posts and reached by a set of stairs. Above the command post stood a lookout tower built of coconut logs which rose fully 25m high.

The returning *chutai* leader quickly gathered his men around him to hear their individual reports of the fight. The IJN had no trained intelligence personnel to conduct mission debriefings at the tactical unit level. No standard procedures existed for assessing victory claims, and much depended on the judgment of individual commanders. Often the claims of combat participants were simply aggregated with little effort made to compensate for possible duplication of claims or overly optimistic assessments.

Having listened to his men, the *chutai* leader stood to attention in front of the command post with his men lined up behind him, all still in flight gear. With the CO and other senior officers of the unit facing him as they stood on the high, open veranda of the command post, the *chutai* leader verbally gave his report. He claimed eight victories in total for his *chutai*: six "Grummans", as the Japanese typically referred to the F4F, and two dive bombers. Five Grummans and one dive bomber were definite victories, he said. One Grumman and one dive bomber were reported as "indefinite" victories, the Japanese equivalent of the Allied "probable". Both had been fired upon and hits observed, but both had ducked into cloud leaving a thin trail of smoke.

But the *chutai* had paid for their victories with two of their own. F 2/C Hasegawa had been hit in a classic bounce from above and behind by the Grummans and went down in a ball of fire before anyone had a chance to react. Nobody noticed the other loss, F 1/C Endo. He simply failed to turn up at the rendezvous point following combat.

Having finished his preliminary verbal report, the *chutai* leader saluted. The CO returned the salute, and, with a few short words of appreciation for their work, dismissed the men. A formal written report of the action (*Sento Yoho*) would be prepared by the staff warrant officer that evening and its essential details entered in the unit's Combat Log (*Sento Kodo Chosho*).

With the crowd dispersing, Hattori now paid a visit to the latrine. This was one of the unexpectedly pleasant amenities on the base. Unlike the putrid, open-pit cesspools usually dug by Japanese forces, the latrine here was built on a platform over a small river which ran along the eastern side of the airstrip. All human waste was automatically flushed away in the stream. But there was one drawback. One had to keep a lookout for crocodiles lurking in the waters of Bougainville. With the latrine platform no more than a meter off the surface of the water, this was no laughing matter.

Having finished his business at the latrine without incident, Hattori was walking back to the airfield when he heard the distinct sound of a *Sakae* engine in the distance. Rushing back to the airstrip along with others who had also heard it, he saw a single *Rei-sen* approaching for a landing. Everyone quickly realized it was Endo, the missing man from the fourth shift over the convoy. He had returned after all! Endo lowered his flaps and undercarriage, pulled back his canopy and managed to raise his seat in preparation for landing. His wings, however, wobbled precariously on final approach, indicating damage or that he was wounded. He managed to get down in one piece and switch off his engine as the crowd came chasing after him on the ground. But having come to a stop at the end of the runway, he clearly struggled to leave the cockpit. F 1/C Sato was first on the scene. Endo was his friend and classmate from *Yokaren* days. Sato clambered up onto the Zero's wing, reached into the cockpit and began gently to undo the wounded pilot's harness straps. Others now rushed up to help. Together they lifted Endo out of the cockpit and onto a waiting stretcher.

Endo had violated a cardinal rule of air combat. Intent on chasing a Grumman fighter, he had lost sight of his *shotai* leader and had strayed too close to the enemy airfield on Guadalcanal. A burst of ground fire had sent shrapnel ripping into his back and side. Fortunately, his bulky, kapok-filled life jacket had cushioned the blows to some extent, and a quick examination by the medical officer at the field hospital showed that no vital organs had been hit. After Endo had recovered some of his strength, the medical officer operated on him to remove the shrapnel and sow up his wounds. There was no anesthesia. Sato and several others held him down on the table while Endo did his best not to scream. The pain was worse than getting wounded in the first place, but Endo survived.

That evening, FPO 1/C Hattori took a bath in one of the fuel drums set up for that purpose near the NCO and enlisted pilots' tent area. The metal cylinder was filled with water and heated from beneath. It was crude but effective, and gave the kind of good hot soak so dear to the hearts of the Japanese. Shortly after his wash, Kimura and Hashimoto came over to tell him that dinner was ready. They had just finished peeling and boiling a mountain of potatoes. Strict observance of rank continued to be a part of daily life, even at this far-flung outpost. Because of their low rank, the junior enlisted men were still expected to help out with mundane chores on the ground. They were not given any special consideration by virtue of their status as pilots.

The single exception to this strict adherence to rank and seniority occurred in the air. Here experience and skill counted for everything. Particularly as attrition took its toll, it was not unknown for a seasoned enlisted flyer to have a newly arrived petty officer on his wing. Past combat experience alone was no guarantee of success in the unforgiving skies of the "Southern Front", particularly if the pilot had been away from front-line duty for sometime. Two weeks previously, a veteran petty officer who had shot down several enemy aircraft in China had gone missing in action along with his two wingmen. The men of the unit had given this NCO due respect in deference to his seniority and past experience. But he had spent the intervening time between his duty in China and his posting to Hattori's unit as a training instructor in Japan. Rather than ask for advice from others who had preceded him here, this veteran seemed more concerned about living up to his reputation, and he was not particularly well liked by the men of the unit. By the time he realized that air combat over the Solomon Island was very different from what he had known in China several years before, it was too late. He had penetrated too far into enemy airspace on a "lone wolf" pursuit and, presumably, had dragged himself and his wingmen to their deaths.

Under normal circumstances, however, it was the more senior pilots who naturally had more experience. Kimura and Hashimoto were happy, at least, that they were now flying combat missions. The more recent arrivals waited for a long time before their names would appear on the mission roster blackboard in front of the command post. Although the new arrivals did not appreciate it, this was due to the care and consideration of senior officers who wished to make sure that the novice pilots were given a smooth introduction to combat in order to build their confidence. But this also meant that a commensurately higher burden fell on the shoulders of the seasoned veterans. This eventually brought on fatigue and greater susceptibility to tropical disease. Hattori himself had been on continuous operations for over a month, and that night he finally succumbed to malaria.

Too weak to drag himself to the slit trench behind his tent when the air raid alarm sounded, he remained on his wooden plank bed as an enemy bomber droned overhead, occasionally dropping a bomb to keep everyone awake. His squadron mates had been attempting to make night interceptions in their *Rei-sen* with the aid of searchlights, but to no avail. Everyone wished for an effective night fighter to counter these nocturnal nuisance raids. Fortunately for Hattori, none of the bombs fell close by.

Two weeks later, although not fully recovered, Hattori was back on operations. There were too few experienced pilots, and his services were urgently needed. By then, Kimura was dead, shot down by F4Fs over Guadalcanal the week before. Sato had been badly wounded on that same mission and was about to be sent back to Japan, one of the lucky few who would leave the "Southern Front" with his life intact. Endo, on the other hand, had just returned to the flight line, having now recovered from his wounds. And, against all odds, Hashimoto had shot down his first enemy aircraft and was on his way to becoming a seasoned pilot.

GLOSSARY

Bakugeki-ki	Bomber. IJN term specifically indicating aircraft with dive bombing capability.
Chutai	Tactical formation consisting of nine aircraft (three *shotai*) for much of IJN history. Later, for fighter formations during 1944–45, a formation of 16 aircraft.
Daitai	Tactical formation consisting of 27 aircraft (three *chutai*) for much of IJN history.
Encho kyoiku	Extended education. IJN term for advanced flight training.
Gekitsui-oh	Literally "shoot-down king". Japanese term roughly equivalent to the Western term "ace".
Hei-shu Hiko Yoka Renshu Sei	C-class Flight Reserve Trainee.
Hentai	A generic term meaning "formation", but the term was specifically used during 1944–45 for tactical formations consisting of a two-plane element adopted by IJN fighters during the latter half of the Pacific War.
Hiko Gakusei	Flight Student. Term used for naval academy graduate flight trainees.
Hiko Renshu Sei	Flight Trainee. Term used for non-commissioned and enlisted flight trainees. Abbreviation *Hiren*.

Hiko Yoka Renshu Sei Flight Reserve Trainee. Abbreviation *Yokaren*.

Hineri-komi Literally "twisting-in". Corkscrew loop maneuver developed by IJN fighter pilots.

Hiren Abbreviation for *Hiko Renshu Sei*.

Kanbaku Abbreviation for *Kanjo Bakugeki-ki*. Shipboard (i.e. carrier-based) bomber (i.e. dive bomber).

Kanko Abbreviation for *Kanjo Kogeki-ki*. Shipboard (i.e. carrier-based) attack aircraft (i.e. torpedo bomber).

Kansen Abbreviation for *Kanjo Sento-ki*. Shipboard (i.e. carrier-based) fighter.

Kantei Abbreviation for *Kanjo Teisatsu-ki*. Shipboard (i.e. carrier-based) reconnaissance aircraft.

Kikan-ju Machine gun.

Kikan-ho Machine cannon.

Kogeki-ki Attack aircraft. IJN term specifically indicating aircraft with torpedo bombing capability.

Koku Sentai Within the IJN's administrative table of organization, the level immediately above a single vessel whose primary purpose was to carry aircraft (such as an aircraft carrier or seaplane tender), or a single *kokutai*. It usually consisted of two or more such vessels or two or more *kokutai*. Usually translated as "carrier division" when aircraft carriers were involved, and as "air flotilla" when *kokutai* were involved.

Kokutai The main operational unit within the administrative table of organization for the IJN Air Service. Excluded were aircraft-carrying ships of the fleet, including aircraft carriers until 1944.

Ko-shu Hiko Yoka A-class Flight Reserve Trainee.

Renshu Sei Kutai Term used during the latter half of Pacific War to refer to a four-plane tactical formation adopted by IJN fighters.

Otsu-shu Hiko Yoka Renshu Sei B-class Flight Reserve Trainee.

Otsu-shu (Toku) Hiko B-class (Special) Flight Reserve Trainee.

Yoka Renshu Sei Rikko Abbreviation for *Rikujo Kogeki-ki*. Land-based attack aircraft.

Sento Kodo Chosho Combat log. Daily record of operational missions flown, and kept at the *kokutai* level. Primarily maintained for the purpose of personnel evaluation.

Sento Yoho Detailed combat report. Action report prepared after significant combat.

Shotai Tactical formation consisting of three aircraft for much of IJN history. Later, for fighter formations during 1944–45, a formation of eight aircraft (two *kutai*).

Soh-ju Renshu Sei Pilot Trainee. Abbreviation Sohren.

Sohren Abbreviation for *Soh-ju Renshu Sei*.

Yokaren Abbreviation for *Hiko Yoka Renshu Sei*.

BIBLIOGRAPHY

Genda Minoru, *Kaigun Kokutai Shimatsu-ki* (Bungei Shunju, 1961)

Iwai Tsutomu, *Kuhbo Rei-sen Tai* (Konnichi No Wadai Sha, 1979)

204 Ku Senshi Kanko Kai, *Rabaul – Dai 204 Kaigun Kokutai Senki* (Kojinsha, 1976)

Ohtawa Tatsuya, *Yokaren Ichidai* (Kojinsha, 1978)

Okumiya Masatake, *Saraba Kaigun Kokutai* (Asahi Sonorama, 1979)

Shimakawa Masaaki, *Rei-sen Kuh-sen Kiroku* (Kojinsha, 1989)

Terai Hozo et al, *Koku Gijutsu No Zenbo* (Nippon Shuppan Kyodo K.K., 1955)

Tsunoda Kazuo, *Shura No Tsubasa* (Konnichi No Wadai Sha, 1988)

COLOR PLATE COMMENTARY

A: The First Shanghai Incident

On 22 February 1932, during the brief three-month conflict between Japan and China known as the First Shanghai Incident, the Imperial Japanese Naval Air Service achieved its first combat victory in the air. Aeroplanes from the aircraft carrier *Kaga*, three Type 3 Mark 2 Carrier Fighters (A1N2) escorting an equal number of Type 13 Mark 3 Carrier Attack Aircraft (3MT2/B1M3), temporarily land-based at Shanghai, managed to shoot down a lone Chinese fighter, the Boeing Model 218, flown by American volunteer pilot Robert M. Short, over Soochow. The Type 13 Attack Aircraft were led by Lieutenant Susumu Kotani, flying as observer in the middle seat of the lead Type 13. The Type 3 Fighters were led by Lieutenant Nogiji Ikuta, his wingmen being APO 3/C Toshio Kuroiwa (No. 2) and A 1/C Kazuo Takeo (No. 3).

1 The Type 13 Attack Aircraft first spotted the Boeing 1,000m ahead and to their right, climbing towards them from an altitude of about 300m. The Type 13s were at an altitude of about 900m, with the Type 3 Fighters above and to their rear at a height of 1,500m.

2 The Type 13s tightened their formation and turned left in order to bring the concentrated fire of their rear-facing 7.7mm machine guns to bear as Robert Short approached, while A 1/C Takeo, the No. 3 wingman in Lieutenant Ikuta's fighter *shotai* dived down to the right to engage the Boeing. Takeo opened fire from a distance of 200m but achieved no telling hits.

3 Meanwhile, Short opened fire on the Type 13s from 500m, then climbed above them, looped and came back to attack from above and to the left rear. In the exchange of fire that followed, Lieutenant Kotani was killed aboard his aircraft, the first combat fatality in the IJN air service, and the wireless operator/gunner, A 1/C Sasaki was wounded.

Meal time was short, but gave respite from the hectic routines of the day. Enlisted and non-commissioned ranks in the IJN lived on a staple of barley rice. Pure rice was a luxury reserved for warrant and commissioned officers. (via Edward M. Young)

4 Short pressed his attack to a distance of 20m from the Type 13s, then passed no more than 10m below Kotani's aircraft and zoomed upwards to the right. At this point he was caught by Lieutenant Ikuta attacking from above and behind, and by APO 3/C Kuroiwa attacking from below, both Japanese fighters opening fire at a distance of 100 to 200m. Ikuta's shots appear to have been decisive. He saw Robert Short pitch forward in his cockpit and observed gasoline vapor stream back from his aeroplane. In the next instant the Boeing went into a vertical dive, caught fire and went down to crash in a right-hand spin.

As Ikuta himself was later to state, the tactics used by his *shotai* on this occasion were a faithful application of fighter doctrine that Lieutenant Yoshio Kamei had studied in Great Britain and which he had subsequently taught to his colleagues in the IJN air service during 1929 following his return to Japan. This first confirmed aerial victory of the Imperial Japanese Naval Air Service, involving a tight three-plane "vic" formation and the subsequent maneuvers of the three fighter pilots, is a classic illustration of the British influence on the early development of IJN aerial tactics.

B: The "hineri-komi" and IJN flying formations

1 The *hineri-komi* or "twisting-in" maneuver, was a corkscrew loop technique initially developed by APO 1/C Isamu Mochizuki at Yokosuka *Kokutai* during 1934. This maneuver involved putting one's fighter at an oblique angle while climbing up in a loop, causing the fighter to face sideways at the top of the loop as it approached the edge of a stall and then execute a corkscrew as it descended out of the loop. This cut down on turning radius and quickly allowed a fighter pilot to obtain an attacking position above and behind an opponent who executed a standard loop. Considerable piloting skill, however, was required to execute this maneuver properly. Used particularly during the early phases of the China War which began in 1937, the *hineri-komi* allowed fighter pilots of the IJN to maintain an edge in classic dogfights against their Chinese opponents flying inherently more maneuvrable aircraft. In the early months of the Pacific War, this maneuver was one of the main factors in establishing the reputation of the IJN fighter pilot as a superb dogfighter. The illustration shows a Type 96 Carrier Fighter (A5M) using the *hineri-komi* against a Chinese Curtiss Hawk III.

2 Standard IJN fighter formations of *chutai* (nine planes) and *daitai* (27 planes). As a rule, even-numbered positions were on the leader's left, while odd-numbered positions were on the right. Thus the basic *shotai* of three aircraft had the No. 2 wingman on the leader's left and the No. 3 wingman on his right, and this arrangement was repeated in progressively larger formations. In a nine-plane *chutai*, therefore, the second *shotai* of three planes flew to the left of the lead *shotai* and the third *shotai* flew on the lead *shotai*'s right. A distance of about two to three plane lengths separated each *shotai*. In a *daitai*, the second *chutai* of nine flew to the left of the lead *chutai* and the third *chutai* flew to the right of the lead *chutai*. A distance of 100 to 150m separated each *chutai*. The two *chutai* on the wings were positioned higher than the lead *chutai*, with the third *chutai* on the right flying top cover.

3 The formations described above came to be reserved for long-distance cruising when combat was not anticipated. Experience in China demonstrated to the Japanese that the tight "vic" formation lacked flexibility in actual combat. They soon adopted a looser formation whenever action was expected, with the No. 2 wingman positioned 20 to 30m to the rear on the leader's left at an angle of 45 degrees to the leader and stationed about 30m higher than the leader, while the No. 3 wingman took up a position about 50m to the rear on the leader's right at an angle of 30 degrees from the leader and approximately 30m higher than the No. 2 man on the left. Sharp left turns while in this configuration required a crossover maneuver among the wingmen which left the No. 2 man on the leader's right and the No. 3 man on his left.

During the Pacific War, progressively from mid-1943 onward, IJN fighters finally came to adopt four-plane formations already long established by their Luftwaffe allies and their American opponents. The IJN air service was probably the last major air force of World War II to adopt the four-plane fighter formation as standard practice.

C: Equipment circa 1937

The basic equipment of the IJN airman changed little during the 1937–45 period. The figure at the top (1) shows the outfit of a trainee pilot around 1937 with a standard kapok-filled life jacket (2), leather flight gauntlets (3) and fur-lined leather flight helmet (4) with a voice-tube attached to the ear flap for communication with his instructor. His flight goggles (5) are of an older type with flat lenses and a flat upper portion to the frame, which was used up to the early years of the China War.

The bottom figure (6) shows a typical IJN pilot during the first half of the Pacific War. Like the upper figure, he wears a winter-issue sheepskin leather helmet (7) lined with rabbit fur. The flight goggles (8) have changed to a model with larger curved lenses, which came into use during the China War and remained standard issue throughout most of the Pacific War. The pilot also wears an 8mm Nambu pistol (9) secured with a rope lanyard and tucked into the belt surrounding his life jacket. This was issued to airmen on overseas duty. The kapok life jacket (10) remains the same as for the upper figure. Note the personal name and unit assignment written on the back of the life jacket. Also shown in the kit breakout is a flight clock (11) worn around the neck on operations. The leather flight gauntlets (12) remain the same as for the upper figure.

Purely a personal adornment and not part of the official kit is a *sen-nin bari* ("a belt of a thousand stitches") (13). This was a traditional talisman dating from the samurai era which was popular with Japanese servicemen during the war years. Intended to ward off bodily harm, much like a lucky rabbit's foot in the West, it was produced by women back home for servicemen at the front by collecting stitches with a needle and thread on a bolt of cotton cloth from passers-by until a thousand had been collected. The recipient wore it wrapped around his waist under his clothes.

Both upper and lower figures wear a one-piece gabardine winter flight suit, quilted on the inside. For seriously cold weather, airmen used a fur-lined suit with fur collar. Electrically heated suits were also used during the Pacific War.

D: Standard *Rikko* formations

1 and **2** Standard Rikko (land-based attack aircraft) formations used from the China War through to the first half of the Pacific War when large daylight missions were being flown. A chutai of nine aircraft (1) and a daitai of 27 (2) are shown in a standard "V of V" formation for horizontal bombing. Note that all aircraft in each shotai, each shotai in a chutai, and each chutai in the daitai are evenly spaced from each other to provide the tightest concentration of bomb pattern possible. Each wingman in relation to his leader, and each wing formation in relation to its lead formation, maintained a slightly higher altitude in order to avoid turbulence from the prop wash of the leader.

3 For defense against enemy fighters the rikko adopted a line-abreast formation in order to bring the highest concentration of defensive fire to bear at any given point along the formation. The transition from a "V of V" formation to a line-abreast was achieved by each wingman moving forward closer to his leader and each wing formation doing the same in relation to their lead formations. Also seen here is this formation shown from the front (3a) and from above (3b).

E: An IJN torpedo attack and dive bombing methods

1 The prescribed method of attack for torpedo bombers, known as *kogeki-ki* or "attack aircraft" in IJN terminology, was to approach the target in a shallow dive and level off for the actual torpedo run at a distance of about 3,000m from the target. The torpedo would be released within 1,000m of the target at a height of about 20m from the surface.

2 It required a practised eye to determine the proper angle of release based on a quick estimate of the target ship's course. Following torpedo release, the only available course for the aircraft was to continue toward the target ship at minimum altitude, below the level of the ship's deck, and hurdle over the ship at the last minute, skimming over the waves again on the other side. It was inevitable that casualties would be high.

3 In contrast to attack aircraft, which were capable of carrying torpedoes as well as bombs but which lacked dive bombing capability, dive bombers in the IJN were referred to specifically as *bakugeki-ki* or "bomber". Approaching the target from higher altitude in a shallow dive, the actual push over into the diving attack itself would occur at an altitude of 4,500–5,000m with bomb release and pull-out beginning at about 450m. At a velocity of 300 knots the aircraft would "sink" a further 300–350m following initiation of pull-out, thus allowing full recovery from the dive at an altitude of about 100m. Veteran crews, however, would sometimes hold their dive until about 300m, confident in their ability to pull out with very little margin to spare. Preferred diving angles in the IJN ranged from about 55 to 60 degrees.

The standard main bomb load for the Type 99 *Kanbaku* (D3A "Val") was 250kg. This was increased to 500kg for its successor, the *Suisei* (D4Y "Judy").

By the start of the Pacific War, torpedo bomber as well as dive bomber crews in the IJN were well practised in coordinating their respective methods of attack against a target ship, not only among the planes from a single carrier, but in conjunction with planes from other carriers in a massed attack. Within their own respective methods of attack, they were also trained to attack their target simultaneously from different directions.

F: Inside a Type I Land-based Attack Aircraft (G4M1) on operations during the Pacific War

1 The forward cockpit scene shows a *Rikko* crew on a search mission. The crewmen wear their flight gear over light khaki tropical fatigues of short-sleeved shirt and short trousers. The junior observer/navigator on the left scans the ocean horizon with binoculars for signs of enemy shipping while the senior observer/aircraft commander eats a lunch of *onigiri* (rice balls) wrapped in *nori* (dried seaweed). The mess orderlies did their best to come up with appealing meals for the aircrew despite limited resources at the front, and the in-flight meal was often the highlight of long, arduous missions for the aircrew. They were often packed in handy-sized portions for the convenience of the crew who could then eat without taking off their flight gauntlets. Ahead of the aircraft commander sits the lead pilot with the co-pilot sitting to his left. This was the opposite of American practice as well as the practice in Japanese army bombers in which the lead pilot sat on the left with the co-pilot on his right.

2 The rear fuselage scene shows the gunners at their stations in action against enemy interceptors. Note that the

Here the floatplane version of the Type 93 Intermediate Trainer (K5Y2) is seen in a formation take-off.

waist gunners must kneel in order to fire their weapons. The rear half of the waist gun blister is shown in its stowed position behind the gunner. Except for the tail gunner who wielded a Type 99 Mark 1 20mm weapon, all defensive armament on the G4M1 were Type 92 7.7mm Machine Guns which proved woefully inadequate against Allied fighters during the Pacific War.

G: Rabaul

Model 52 *Rei-sen* (A6M5) from aircraft carrier *Zuikaku* in action over Rabaul, New Britain on November 2 1943 against P-38s and B-25s of the Fifth Air Force, USAAF.

On the previous day, some 170 *kansen* (carrier fighters), *kanbaku* (carrier bombers), *kanko* (carrier attack aircraft) and *kantei* (carrier reconnaissance planes) from the 1st *Koku Sentai* composed of the aircraft carriers *Shokaku*, *Zuikaku* and *Zuiho*, flew into airfields at Rabaul and Kavieng, New Ireland, for a round of strikes on Allied aircraft and shipping in the region. Early on the morning of the 2nd, a large part of this force sortied against American warships and transports around Bougainville, but upon returning to Rabaul, these airmen were still spoiling for a fight. While rearming and refueling for another mission, the Rabaul area received a sudden low-level attack by over 150 B-25s and P-38s of the Fifth Air Force flying from New Guinea bases. The Japanese detected the fast-approaching American planes at the last minute, and a wild scramble followed as the *Rei-sen* took off to intercept. In total, 115 fighters (58 from the 1st *Koku Sentai*, together with 57 of their land-based unit colleagues from 204, 201, and 253 *Kokutai*) gave the men of the Fifth Air Force an unexpectedly hot reception on that date. The Japanese shot down nine B-25s and ten P-38s although they lost 18 of their own number in the action.

Here, *Rei-sen* from the *Zuikaku* fighter unit engage strafer-modified B-25Ds of the 501st Bomb Squadron, 345th Bomb Group, as they head for the outer harbor following their attack along the eastern shore of Simpson Harbor. P-38Gs of the 80th Fighter Squadron, 8th Fighter Group, which had earlier swept ahead of the bombers, engage the *Rei-sen*. In the background, following squadrons of B-25s begin to attack shipping in the harbor. Smoke rises from Rabaul town and the wharf area along the western shore as a result of earlier attacks. A couple of No. 3 aerial-burst phosphorous bombs dropped on the American formation by Japanese interceptors add to the smoke and confusion of other phosphorous bombs dropped earlier by the American bombers on some of their targets.

Many men of the Fifth Air Force remember November 2 1943 as the toughest single action they fought during the entire Pacific War and refer to it as "Bloody Tuesday". This battle proved that, although now clearly on the defensive, the fighter pilots of the IJN were still formidable opponents at this juncture of the war in the Pacific.

H: Equipment circa 1945

Late-war IJN pilot and his kit. Little has changed from earlier years. The flight helmet (1) is a late-war Type 3 with aluminium cups for radio earphones built into the ear flaps. The helmet also has a strap attached to the top of the helmet for the radio wire and an attachment on the right side (not shown) for the radio wire and plug. It also has attachment loops for an oxygen mask. This type of helmet was used to a very limited extent by the IJN at the end of the war. Late-war flight goggles (2) were standardised with those used by army airmen and had ventilation holes along the sides of the lenses. Although the Nambu pistol remained standard issue (3), they were used only on overseas duty and were not carried by airmen on homeland defence.

The figure is attired in a two-piece gabardine summer flight suit buttoned at the front. The buttons on the sleeves indicate continued use of older-issue kit. Later flight suits had zippered sleeves. Note also the name patch sewn onto his left breast. A silk scarf, often salvaged from an old parachute, was widely used by IJN airmen. The rubber-heeled black leather flying boots (4) remained standard throughout the war years as shown here as well as on the figures in Plate C. The Japanese flag *hinomaru* patch on his upper sleeve was added for better identification following an incident on 17 February 1945 in which a Japanese civilian mob, in the mistaken belief that they were attacking an enemy airman, killed an IJN pilot who had bailed out following combat over the homeland.

Items 5, the standard kapok-filled life jacket, and 6, the leather flight gauntlets, did not change from the ones issued at the start of the war (shown also on plate C).

INDEX

Figures in **bold** refer to illustrations.